BEEKEEF

SWARM:

A

BEEKEEPING AND THE LAW
SWARMS AND NEIGHBOURS
A CASE-BOOK

J. David Frimston Ll.B. N.D.B.
Fellow of the British Beekeepers Association
Solicitor
and
His Honour Judge David Smith Q.C.
Hon. Secretary International Bee Research Association

Illustrated with
woodcuts by
Miriam MacGregor

BEE BOOKS NEW & OLD
Tapping Wall Farm, Burrowbridge, Somerset

Introduction, Notes and Appendices
by
J.D.Frimston & David Smith 1993
©
ISBN 0 905652 25 8

ACKNOWLEDGEMENTS

We are grateful to the following for their kind permission to reproduce the law reports contained herein. In addition to those mentioned below we are grateful to many others for giving us notes of cases and other help. We would like to mention in particular His Honour Judge Goodman, Morgan Lewis & Bockius, Counselors at Law and the Newark and Sherwood District Council.

      Bee Craft Ltd, Whitstable,Kent.
      Butterworths, London.
      New Zealand Council of Law Reporting, Wellington, New Zealand.
      The Incorporated Council of Law Reporting for England and Wales.
      The Incorporated Council of Law Reporting for Ireland., Dublin.
      The New Law Journal, London.
      The Pennsylvania District and County Law Reports, Philadelphia.
      The Law Society of Upper Canada, Le Barreau du Haut-Canada.
      Times Newspapers Ltd., London.

"I would observe that however it may have been anciently, in modern days the bee has become almost as completely domesticated as the ox or the cow."

Mr Justice Selden. New York . 1850

Printed in Great Britain by
Butler & Tanner Ltd.,
Frome, Somerset

CONTENTS

INTRODUCTION

Beekeepers do not often find that their hobby leads them into the law courts, but there is no honey without some stings and the stinging sometimes leads to a dispute with the neighbours. Moreover lawyers know that, if it comes to a real battle, disputes within a family are usually the worst, with disputes between neighbours coming a close second.

The English Common Law applies the doctrine of precedent. That is to say that if a legal point has been decided in a particular way it is usually sensible to apply the same principle in future cases. Cases which involve a decision on an interesting point of law are reported in various series of law reports and such reports are referred to in future cases.

It should therefore be no surprise that there are a number of cases reported in the law reports which deal with disputes between neighbours and the ownership of swarms.

The purpose of this book

This book has two main purposes. In the first place it is intended to be a bee case book, that is to say a book of legal case law that could be used in court. We have included the most important cases on the subject, many of which are contained in law reports that are not readily available. In each case we have included the whole report. There were comments in *Robins v. Kennedy and Columb* and *Ingamells v. Pickford* about the difficulty in obtaining copies of the relevant reports. We hope that this book will solve that particular problem.

However we hope that the book will also be of interest to beekeepers, whether or not they are in dispute with their neighbours, because the cases are interesting in themselves and they often tell a fascinating story. In the case of *O'Gorman* the story is not only interesting but also tragic.

We should explain to the lawyers that we have also included a number of cases which are not, strictly speaking, law reports at all, because they do illustrate the problems involved in such cases, as well as the kind of evidence that may be available.

The Courts

Nowadays if there is a civil claim involving bees in England and Wales it would almost certainly be decided in the County Court by a Circuit Judge sitting alone without a jury. The County Court is bound to follow the decisions of superior English Courts, but if there are no decisions exactly on the point the court would look at similar decisions in other Common Law countries. Such decisions are "persuasive" authorities although not binding. It is therefore relevant to consider law reports from other countries and so cases are quoted from Scotland, Ireland, Canada, New Zealand and the U.S.A. We hope that this book will therefore be of interest to lawyers and beekeepers in those countries as well.

We also include some County Court cases because although such judgments in one County Court are not binding on another Circuit Judge they are similarly "persuasive"

In the past many civil disputes were decided by juries. Nowadays juries are not involved in many civil cases except for libel and a few other cases such as false imprisonment. Some of the cases in this book therefore involve a decision in a higher court as to the correctness of the jury's original decision.

The present law

We have little doubt that a suit brought against a beekeeper by a neighbour who wishes to complain about bees must be founded in negligence or nuisance.

Negligence involves damage caused by negligence to another person to whom one has an obligation to take care. It is perhaps most familiar to non lawyers in cases of road accidents. Anyone who drives on the roads is under a duty to other road users to take care. If he is negligent and causes damage to another he is liable in damages.

Similarly an occupier of land is under a duty not to behave in such a way as to make his neighbour's life impossible. He must not, for example by making noise or smells or vibrations, spoil his neighbour's reasonable enjoyment of the premises next door. Such conduct is described as a nuisance and is actionable.

There is much academic discussion as to the extent to which nuisance also involves negligence. Very often a case is brought which makes both allegations. Certainly in the context of beekeeping it is difficult to imagine a case in nuisance which does not involve negligence. For example if the Plaintiff is complaining about the number of hives, the way in which they are sited and possibly the fact that the bees are of a vicious temperamen, he is claiming that the Defendant's conduct amounts to a nuisance and also that it is caused by the Defendant's negligence.

The old law

Lawyers have a tendency to make a claim in as many ways as possible in the hope that if one point fails another may succeed. The cases therefore include two other attempted causes of action which always failed but we mention them by way of explanation.

The *scienter* action was an action involving strict liability for animals, that is liability whether or not there was any negligence. If a person kept a wild animal like a lion and it escaped and caused damage he was liable for the damage. He would "know" that a lion was likely to cause damage. *Scienter* is simply the Latin word for "knowingly". If a person kept a tame animal but one that he knew was vicious, such as a fierce dog, he was similarly liable. Hence the saying that every dog is entitled to one bite. If he had not bitten before, he was presumed not to be vicious, but once he had bitten somebody the owner knew he might well bite again. This old law has now been replaced by the Animals Act 1971 and, as far as dogs are concerned, by the Dangerous Dogs Act 1991. Attempts were made to use this action against beekeepers in the past but without success. It is most unlikely that any individual bee would sting twice although it is possible to imagine circumstances in which it could be shown that the beekeeper knew his bees were more fierce than other bees. Occasionally beekeepers have been heard to say that they know they have got fierce bees but they believe that fierce bees gather more honey.

The case of *Rylands v. Fletcher* was another action involving strict liability. That was a case where a mill owner had made a reservoir on his land but the water broke through some old mine shafts and flooded the neighbour's mine. The court decided that this accumulation of water involved an unnatural use of land, and, since the landowner had brought on to his land something that was liable to cause damage if it escaped, he was therefore liable for the damage if it did escape, whether or not he was negligent. It has been argued that bees are liable to cause damage if they escape and so this rule should apply. These cases have always failed, mainly because it is difficult to suggest that beekeeping is not a natural use of land.

The ownership of swarms

Nobody would have much hesitation in saying that a beekeeper owns his hives together with the bees inside. Bees are regularly bought and sold on frames or in packages. It is not surprising that there is a Canadian case, *McKay v. Davey* (1913) XXVIII Ontario Law Reports 322, which decided that a beekeeper was liable for damages for breach of contract when he sold bees that were infected with foul brood.

Much of the discussion in the old cases about the ownership of animals revolves around the division of animals into two classes i.e. *ferae naturae* (wild animals) and *domitae naturae* (domesticated animals). This classification has nothing to do with ferocity because doves or rabbits are classified as wild but no one would say they were fierce. In simple terms a man can clearly be said to be the owner of a wild animal while he has it confined in a cage. What if it escapes ? The old law provided that it simply became a wild animal again which was owned by no one. But some wild animals are not usually confined by their owners. Doves, for example, would be expected to fly freely over a neighbours land and then return to the dovecote. In such a case it was said that the animal had an *animus revertendi* (an intention to return) and therefore it still belonged to its owner even when it was not on his land.

It is interesting to apply these principles to bees. An individual bee on a foraging flight clearly has the necessary intention of returning to the hive, or *animus revertendi* as the lawyers would say. On this basis the bee is still the property of the beekeeper. If a neighbour kills foraging bees he is destroying the beekeeper's property, but it is not likely that such a case would ever reach the law courts if only a few bees were involved. Quite apart from the expense of the case, there would be a considerable problem in proving where an individual bee had come from. The issue did arise in *Tutton -v- Walter* [1986] 1 Queens Bench 61 where the plaintiffs claimed damages for losses caused by spraying of oil seed rape. Dennis Henry Q.C. sitting as a deputy High Court Judge noted that it was conceded that the plaintiffs had property in their bees (i.e. they owned the individual bees) sufficient to enable them to bring an action for negligence and referred to Blackstone's Commentaries Book 2 Ch 25 p. 329. *Tutton v. Walter* is too long to include here and is readily available in the Law Reports but we have included the head-note at p. 52.

It is a different matter when bees swarm. Swarming bees do not intend to return to the hive. The question therefore arises as to who owns a swarm of bees in the air or on the branch in a neighbour's garden. There is little doubt that the old practice of "tanging" a swarm by beating various metal objects together had a dual purpose. First it was thought that the vibrations would cause the bees to settle. Secondly the beekeeper was proclaiming to the world at large that these swarming bees were his bees. In various cases it has been argued that in accordance with principles of Roman law the beekeeper is entitled to follow his bees wherever they go. In *Hallett v. Jones* (1935) LXXX Law Journal 173 this point was conceded by the Defendant, probably incorrectly, but it is clear from the later case of *Kearry v. Pattinson* that there is no right to go on to another's land and that the landowner can, if he chooses, take the swarm and keep the bees. The case of *Kearry v. Pattinson* contains much fascinating material from Roman Law, early cases and textbooks and also a long quotation from Blackstone.

We hope this short account of the law will help non lawyers in their understanding of the cases which follow. We suggest that the lawyers consult their textbooks for further exposition.

Finally a few brief points.

All the Law Reports contained in this book have been carefully checked with the originals to make certain that they are full and accurate accounts and can be relied upon for any purpose as completely as if they were the originals.

The Editors' Introductory Notes at the beginning of each report are the responsibility of the Editors and are there to draw the attention of beekeepers and others to the points in the judgments that appear to the Editors to be of importance.

As lawyers will know the foreign cases may in some respects not be correct accounts of the English law on the points they deal with but they are put in to show the way that foreign courts have dealt with very similar problems and to suggest how the same problems might be dealt with here. Similarly reports of past cases in this country must be used with caution as they may not be correct statements of the current law on the subject.

One of the great values of the reports we have collected is to show how the courts judge whether a beekeeper is keeping bees "reasonably" and whether the neighbour is expecting too much in the way of being free from troublesome insects, but there is nothing more difficult than defining "reasonableness".

In deciding which cases to include in this book we have necessarily been selective, although we feel that we can justifiably claim that we have included every case of any real importance. However Appendix 2 lists some other cases on the subject which we have not included. Addicts (or perhaps we should describe them as real enthusiasts) who are anxious to pursue the subject further can ask for copies of these cases, or the address of the publishers of them, from the first named author.

I   1850 USA.
EARL v. VAN ALSTINE
Editors' Introductory Notes

The report contains a clear exposition of the arguments against there being any liability under the scienter action. The plaintiff had won in the court of first instance but he lost on appeal and the Supreme Court affirmed the decision of the Appeal Court

The case is an old one having been decided in 1850 in New York State but it is still quoted in modern digests as an authority.

Selden,J. in his judgment said:-

That the division of animals into those *ferae naturae* and those *domitae naturae* had reference mainly if not entirely to the matter of ownership in them and not to the question whether they were ferocious and savage or not.

That one who owns or keeps an animal of any kind becomes liable for any injury the animal may do only on the ground of some actual or presumed negligence on his part.

That it is essential to the proof of negligence, and sufficient evidence thereof, that the owner be shown to have had notice of the propensity of the animal to do mischief.

That proof that the animal is of a savage and ferocious nature is equivalent to proof of express notice. In such cases notice is presumed.

In modern days the bee has become almost as completely domesticated as the ox or the cow.

It can be controlled and managed with nearly as much certainty as any of the domestic animals.

That such a thing as a *serious* injury to person or property from its attacks is very rare, not occurring in a ratio more frequent certainly than injuries arising from the kick of a horse, or the bite of a dog.

That the law looks with more favour upon the keeping of animals that are useful to man, than such as are purely noxious and useless.

That the owner of bees is not liable *at all events* for any accidental injury they may do. The question whether the keeping of these bees so near the highway subjects the defendant to a responsibility which would not otherwise rest upon him was substantially disposed of by the evidence in the case. It appeared to him that bees had been kept in the same situation for some eight or nine years, and no proof was offered of the slightest injury ever having been done by them.

The Animals Act 1971, the Dangerous Wild Animals Act 1976 and the Dangerous Dogs Act 1991 have altered the position in this country.

Later cases in the United States referred to in 86 ALR3d 830:-
Ferreira v D'Asaro (1963, Fla App D3) 152 So 2d 736.
Parsons v Manser (1903) 119 Iowa, 88 93 NW 86.
Ammons v Kellogg (1925) 137 Miss 551, 102 So 562.
Petey Mfg. Co. v Dryden (1904) 21 Del 166.
Allman v Rexer (1934) 21 Pa D & C 431
Those referred to in 88 ALR3d 995:-
Cox v New Castle County (1970) Del (Sup) 265 .
Olmsted v Rich (1889, Sup) 6 NYS 826.
Whitemarsh Township v Cummings (1956) 7 Pa D & C2d 557.
Holden v Lewis (1946) 56 Pa D & C 639, 33 Del Co 458.

REPORT
OF
EARL v. VAN ALSTINE
(1850) NY 8 Barb 630

Monroe General Term, June , 1850. *Welles, Johnson,* and *Selden*, Justices.

One who owns or keeps an animal, of any kind, becomes liable for any injury the animal may do, only on the ground of some actual or presumed negligence on his part.

It is essential to the proof of negligence, and sufficient evidence thereof, that the owner be shown to have had notice of the propensity of the animal to do mischief.

Proof that the animal is of a savage and ferocious nature, is equivalent to proof of express notice. In such cases notice is presumed.

The owner of *bees* is not liable, *at all events*, for any accidental injury they may do.

Where, in an action against the owner of bees, for an injury done by them to the plaintiff's horses while travelling along the highway past the place where the bees were kept, it appeared that the bees had been kept in the same situation for eight or nine years, and there was no proof of any injury ever having been done by them, but on the contrary, witnesses residing in the neighborhood testified that they had been in the habit of passing and repassing the place frequently, without having been molested; it was held that this rebutted the idea of any notice to the defendant, either from the nature of the bees or otherwise, that it would be dangerous to keep them in that situation; and that he could not be made liable.

THIS action was commenced in a justice's court. The complaint alledged that the defendant was the owner of 15 hives of bees, which he wrongfully kept in his yard adjoining the public highway, and that the plaintiff's horses while travelling along the highway and passing the place where the bees were kept, were attacked and stung so severely that one of them died and the other was greatly injured, &c. The answer denied the charge contained in the complaint. Upon the trial, the keeping of the bees as alledged, and the injury to the horses, were proved, and the plaintiff recovered judgment for $70,25 and costs. Upon appeal to the county court of Wayne county, this judgment was reversed, and the cause was brought to this court by appeal from the judgment of the county court.

By the Court, SELDEN, J. This case presents two questions;
1. Is any one who keeps bees liable, at all events, for the injuries they may do? and 2. Did the defendant keep these bees in an improper manner or place, so as to render him liable on that account?

It is insisted by the plaintiff that while the proprietor of animals of a tame or domestic nature *domitae naturae*, is liable for injuries done by them, (aside from trespasses upon the soil,) only after notice of some vicious habit or propensity of such animal; that one who keeps animals *ferae naturae* is responsible at all events for any injuries they may do, and that as bees belong to the latter class it follows of course that the defendant is liable.

In order to determine this question, upon which no direct or controlling authority exists, that I have been able to find, it becomes necessary to look into the principles upon which one who owns or keeps animals is held liable for their vicious acts. It will be found, on examination of the authorities upon the subject, that this classification of animals by the common law into animals *ferae naturae* and *domitae naturae* has reference mainly if not exclusively, to the rights of property which may be acquired in them; those of the latter class being the subject of absolute and permanent ownership, while in regard to the former only a qualified property can exist, and the distinction is based upon the extent to which they can be domesticated or brought under the control and dominion of man and not at all upon the ferocity of their disposition, or their proneness to mischief. For instance, the dog, some species of which are extremely savage and ferocious, is uniformly classed among animals *domitae naturae*, while the hare, the rabbit and the dove are termed *ferae naturae*, although comparatively harmless. It would not be rational to suppose that a classification adopted with exclusive reference to one quality of animals, could be safely used to define and regulate responsibilities growing out of other and different qualities; nor would it accord with that just analysis and logical accuracy which distinguish the common law, that it should be resorted to for that purpose. And although some dicta may be found in the books which might seem to countenance the idea, the decided cases do not lead to any such conclusion.

It is unnecessary to enter into any examination of the cases which establish one branch of the proposition contended for, to wit, that in order to make the owner of a domestic animal liable for any violent injury done by them unless connected with a trespass upon land, it must be averred and proved that the defendant had notice or knowledge of the mischievous nature of the animal. This, as a general rule, is settled by a series of decisions which have been entirely uniform from the earliest days to the present time. But although in many of these cases, most of which are cases of injuries done by dogs, the words *domitae naturae*, or equivalent words, are used to describe the animals, for the mischief done by which their owners would not be liable without notice, yet it is not alone because they belong to that class that the exemption arises, but because animals of that class are usually of a harmless disposition. I apprehend that if a person chooses to keep a domestic animal, as a dog, which is naturally savage and dangerous, he does so at his peril, and that he would be liable for an injury done by such dog, without evidence that he had ever done mischief before. This position is not without authority to support it, although it does not rest upon any adjudged case. In *Judge v. Cox*, (1 *Stark.* 285) Abbot, J. suggests the question, but expressly reserves his opinion upon it as unnecessary to the decision of that case. But in *Hartley v. Harriman,* (1 *Barn. & Ald.* 620) which was an action for any injury done to sheep by dogs, the declaration contained a special averment that the dogs were accustomed to worry and bite sheep; and the court held that this averment was not supported by proof that the dogs were of a ferocious and mischievous disposition. But Lord Ellenborough and Mr Justice Bayley both said that it would have been sufficient to alledge generally that the dogs were of a ferocious nature, and unsafe to be left at large, and that evidence of that fact would support the action. These dicta are so obviously in accordance with common sense and reason, that they will undoubtedly be sustained whenever the question shall arise. It is true that in a case of injuries done to sheep our statute makes the owner liable without notice, provided the sheep are killed, but the principle would apply to any other injury.

But while, as I have said, the cases which define the responsibilities of the owners of domestic animals are very numerous, those which relate to the liability of the proprietor of wild animals are rare. It has been assumed, rather than decided, that the latter class are kept at the peril of their owners. In *Rex v. Huggins*, (2 *Ld.. Raym.* 1583,) it is said "There is a difference between things *ferae naturae*, as lions, bears, &c. which a man must keep up at his peril, and beasts that are *mansuetae naturae*, and break through the tameness of their nature, such as oxen and horses. In the latter case the owner must have notice; in the former an action lies against the owner without notice." The case in which this was said was an indictment for murder, but the language here given is copied and adopted by Buller, in his Nisi Prius. (*Bull. N.P.* 77) It will be observed that while these authorities speak of a whole class, "things *ferae naturae*," yet the example given is that of lions, bears, &c.

So in a late case in our own courts, *Van Leuven v. Lyke* (1 *Comst.* 516,) Judge Jewett, after stating the rule in respect to domestic animals, says, but as to animals *ferae naturae*, such as lions, tigers and the like, the person who keeps them is liable for any damage they may do, without notice, on the ground that by nature such animals are *fierce* and *dangerous*." Here the learned judge, although adopting the same classification, yet states the true ground of the owner's responsibility. The substance of the rules as given by him is, that one who keeps lions, tigers, or other fierce and dangerous animals, is liable at all events for any injury they may do. The words *ferae naturae* add nothing of any value to the rule, but rather tend to mislead, as they are descriptive of many animals that are not ferocious or dangerous.

Peake, in his work on evidence, under the head of "Actions founded in negligence," has the following: "If one man keep a lion, bear or any other wild and *ferocious* animal, and such animal escape from his confinement and do mischief to another, the owner is liable to make satisfaction for the mischief so done without further evidence of negligence in him; for every person who keeps such noxious and *useless* animals must keep them at his peril. On the contrary, if a man has a dog, a bull, or any other domestic animal such as are usually kept and are indeed *necessary to the existence of man*, no action is maintainable without proof of knowledge, &c.; for without such knowledge no negligence or fault is imputable to the defendant." (*Norris' Peake*, 486.) Three things are worthy of notice in this extract. In the first place the author mentions animals that are not only wild but *ferocious*, and speaks of them as not only noxious but *useless*. In speaking of domestic animals he dwells upon their utility and value; and lastly, he makes negligence the foundation of the liability of the owner.

Again, Chitty, under the head of actions on the case for negligence, gives the rule as follows: "The owner of domestic or other animals, *not naturally inclined to do mischief*, as dogs, horses and oxen, is not liable for any injury committed by them to the person or personal property, unless it can be shown that he previously had notice of the animal's mischievous propensity." (*Chit.Plead.*82.) This accurate elementary writer did not fall into the error of applying the rule to the whole class of animals *domitae naturae*, but adds the qualification "not naturally inclined to do mischief." By his arrangement of the subject, too, he confirms the view of Peake, that the liability is based upon negligence.

These authorities seem to me to point to the following conclusions. 1. That one who owns or keeps an animal of any kind becomes liable for any injury the animal may do, only on the ground of some actual or presumed negligence on his part. 2. That it is essential to the proof of negligence, and sufficient evidence thereof, that the owner be shown to have had notice of the propensity of the animal to do mischief. 3. That proof that the animal is of a savage and ferocious nature is equivalent to proof of express notice. In such cases notice is presumed.

These views derive some support from the case of *May and Wife v. Burdett*, (9 *Adol. & El. N.S.* 101) That was an action on the case, for an injury done to the wife by the bite of a monkey. The declaration alledged that the defendant kept the monkey wrongfully, well knowing that it was of a mischievous and ferocious nature and accustomed to bite, &c.; but did not aver that the defendant had been guilty of any negligence. A verdict was found for the plaintiff, and the defendant moved in arrest of judgment, on the ground that as the action was founded in negligence, the declaration was defective in not containing any averment that the defendant had been guilty of negligence. The motion was overruled, it being after verdict. Ch. J.Denman says, "But the conclusion to be drawn from an examination of all the authorities appears to us to be this, that a person keeping a *mischievous* animal *with knowledge* of its propensities, is bound to keep it secure at his peril, and that if it does mischief *negligence is presumed.* The negligence is in keeping such an animal after notice." The injury for which this action was brought was done by an animal clearly *ferae naturae,* and yet it was deemed necessary to aver the mischievous nature of the animal, together with knowledge on the part of the owner; and the question which arose and was very elaborately discussed was, whether the plaintiff should not have gone still farther, and inserted an averment of negligence.

Having shown then, as I think, clearly, that the liability does not depend upon the classification of the animal doing the injury, but upon its propensity to do mischief, it remains to be considered whether bees are animals of so ferocious a disposition, that every one who keeps them, under any circumstances, does so at his peril. If it is necessary for the plaintiff to aver and prove the mischievous nature of the animal, nothing of the kind was done in this case; but if the courts are to take judicial notice of the nature of things so familiar to man as bees, which I suppose they would be justified in doing, then I would observe that however it may have been anciently, in modern days the bee has become almost as completely domesticated as the ox or the cow. Its habits and its instincts have been studied, and through the knowledge thus acquired it can be controlled and managed with nearly as much certainty as any of the domestic animals; and although it may be proper still to class it among those *ferae naturae,* it must nevertheless be regarded as coming very near the dividing line, and in regard to its propensity to mischief, I apprehend that such a thing as a *serious* injury to person or property from its attacks is very rare, not occurring in a ratio more frequent certainly than injuries arising from the kick of a horse, or the bite of a dog.

There is one rule to be extracted from the authorities to which I have referred, not yet noticed, and that is that the law looks with more favor upon the keeping of animals that are useful to man, than such as are purely noxious and useless. And the keeping of the one, although in some rare instances they may do injury, will be tolerated and encouraged, while there is nothing to excuse the keeping of the other. In the case of *Vrooman v. Lawyer, (*13 *John. Rep.*339,) the court say "If damage be done by any domestic animal kept for use or convenience, the owner is not liable to an action, without notice." The utility of bees no one will question, and hence there is nothing to call for the application of a very stringent rule to the case. Upon the whole, therefore, I am clearly of the opinion that the owner of bees is not liable *at all events* for any accidental injury they may do. The question is still left whether the keeping of these bees so near the highway subjects the defendant to a responsibility which would not otherwise rest upon him. I consider this question as substantially disposed of by the evidence in the case. It appears that bees had been kept in the same situation for some eight or nine years, and no proof was offered of the slightest injury ever having been done by them. On the contrary, some of the witnesses testify that they had lived in the neighborhood and had been in the habit of passing and repassing frequently, with teams and otherwise, without ever having been molested. This rebuts the idea of any notice to the defendant, either from the nature of bees or otherwise, that it would be dangerous to keep them in that situation; and of course, upon the principles already settled, he could not be held liable.

The judgment of the county court must be affirmed.

II	**1903. Ireland.**

O'GORMAN v. O'GORMAN

Editors' Introductory Notes.

This is a well-known and often quoted case. The jury seem to have shown a good deal of common sense and to have understood the behaviour and habits of bees. The beekeeper had behaved very badly and without any sympathy for the neighbour who suffered greatly from the event and died later from his injuries. The haggard referred to in the report was a stack yard for hag etc. It is not clear whether the damages were awarded for the nuisance or for the plaintiff's injuries.

The jury said that the bees were kept negligently; in an unreasonable number and in an unreasonable place and with appreciable danger to the neighbours; they were of a dangerous and mischievous nature; the honey was not taken from the hive with reasonable care, skill and prudence.

The jury found that the defendant had set up an actionable nuisance. Kenny, J. said that he did not think that the finding could be quarrelled with.

Barton, J. did not think that the verdict could be supported on the ground of scienter; nor on the ground of nuisance or unreasonable user of land.

He considered that if the verdict could be supported, it must be by reference to the facts and findings of the jury as to negligence.

He also quoted the definition of negligence when he said:- "If one man is near to another, or is near to the property of another, a duty lies upon him not to do that which may cause a personal injury to that other, or may injure his property".

He said the case could not be represented as a mere case of a man who had been injured in consequence of a sting. If that was all, there could be no duty and no liability.

But he said a "smoker" is an instrument which, when applied to beehives, is, of such a character that it may cause injury to a person who is near, unless some precautions are taken.

Was it unreasonable to come to the conclusion that there was some duty cast upon defendant towards his neighbour to warn him or take some other precaution?

Once negligence is established, it is no answer that the damage, if it followed the natural course of things, was more serious than was or might have been expected.

REPORT

Of

O'GORMAN v. O'GORMAN

[1903] 2 I.R. 573   Before KENNY, BARTON, and WRIGHT, JJ.
(1901. No.5575.)   K.B. DIV. 1902 Nov 20. 21.

Negligence-Bees-Kept in unreasonable numbers and at an unreasonable place-Negligence in the management of beehives-Smoking hives,with knowledge of danger to those in the immediate neighbourhood-Remoteness of damage.

Plaintiff and defendant resided on adjacent farms. Defendant, who was a farmer acquainted with the ways and management of bees and horses, placed and kept upwards of twenty beehives at some distance from his own stables and farmyard, at the boundary fence beside plaintiff's yard and haggard. The bees swarming from these hives frequently caused annoyance to, and gave rise to complaints from, the inhabitants of the farm upon which plaintiff resided. On the occasion in question defendant proceeded to the hives for the purpose of removing honey, and for that purpose smoked the hives with a "smoker". For his own protection he wore a crape veil and a suit of sting-proof garments. There was evidence that he knew, or ought to have known, that plaintiff was likely to be tackling his horse at this very spot, and that his horse was there, but he did not warn plaintiff, or take any other precaution on his account. Numbers of bees, irritated by the smoking operation, swarmed upon plaintiff and his horse. The horse stung by the bees, dragged plaintiff and threw him violently against a wall, causing very severe injuries to his spine. The jury found that plaintiff's injuries were caused by the bees having stung plaintiff and his horse; that they were kept on defendant's land negligently, in unreasonable numbers, at an unreasonable place, and with appreciable danger to the inhabitants of the adjoining farm; that the bees were, to the knowledge of defendant, of a dangerous and mischievous nature, and accustomed to sting mankind and domestic animals; and that the honey was not taken from the hive on the occasion in question with reasonable care, skill, and prudence; and returned a general verdict for the plaintiff, with £200 damages:-

Held, that, having regard to the special facts of the case and findings of the jury, the verdict ought not to be disturbed.

Held, also, that the damage was not too remote.

ACTION for damages inflicted by bees. The plaintiff Patrick O'Gorman was the son of a farmer residing at Gurtnalougha in the County Clare. The defendants Peter O'Gorman and Michael O'Gorman, father and son, were farmers occupying land adjoining that of the plaintiff's father. Some years prior to the month of September, 1900, the defendant Michael O'Gorman placed two straw beehives on his lands, and the number was increased year by year until upon the date in question there were in a row from fourteen to twenty beehives of various descriptions at the boundary fence of, and in close proximity to, the dwellinghouse and haggard of the plaintiff's father. Complaints had been made upon two or three occasions by the plaintiff and his father to the defendants of annoyance caused by the swarming of the bees. Men engaged in haymaking were obliged to cease working, and shortly before the date of the occurrence in question the plaintiff who had been attacked while digging potatoes, complained to the defendant Peter O'Gorman, whose observation in reply was, "Are they prodding you?" Upon the 20th September, 1900, about mid-day, the plaintiff brought a horse into the farmyard near the boundary fence where the beehives were placed, and close up to the door of his father's dwelling-house, for the purpose of harnessing the horse. This was his usual time and place for harnessing the horse. The harness, which was in the kitchen, was handed to him by his mother. He had put on the winkers and long reins, and was putting on the collar and harness when a swarm of bees came across the low wall and whitethorn hedge which separated the two farm premises. Many of the bees perched on the horse, which immediately took fright, and as it started and turned Plaintiff's foot caught in the reins. He was thrown against a low wall and was crushed against it by the head and breast of the horse. His back was bent over the wall. He endeavoured to get into the cow-house, but he was knocked down again by the horse at the gable of the dwellinghouse. The horse then escaped from the haggard. The plaintiff at the time felt his back slightly hurt, the sight was taken from his eyes, and he was badly stung by the bees.

The bees that swarmed into plaintiff's yard and stung plaintiff and his horse, were at the time driven from the neighbourhood of the hives by a "smoker" which was being applied to some of the hives by Michael O'Gorman, with the object of removing honey. The defendant admitted that he knew the danger of such an operation to persons in the immediate neighbourhood. He wore a large hat and a crape veil over his face; he had his hands covered and a cloak thrown over his body, all as protection against the viciousness (or stinging) of the bees. Defendant admitted that he knew that plaintiff was in the habit of coming to that place to tackle his horse, and that he saw the horse there and on previous occasions, and it was proved that this was the usual time for plaintiff to come there to tackle his horse. It was stated that after the plaintiff was thrown down the defendant was called to by plaintiff's mother to come to plaintiff's assistance, but that he answered that he had not time.

About a fortnight afterwards the plaintiff became weak and went to the Clare Infirmary. He attended the trial, which took place before Mr Justice Johnson and a jury at Limerick Spring Assizes, 1902 and gave evidence on his own behalf. The medical evidence given in support of his case was to the effect that he was suffering from conditions which would have been produced by the spine being acutely bent and the cord or membrane injured when forced on the wall. Medical evidence was given for the defendants to the effect that his condition was due to disease on both sides of the spine, and not to external injury inflicted at so recent a date as the 20th September, 1900. The defendants' ownership of the hives was also denied, it being alleged that when defendant Michael O'Gorman was appointed cess collector in 1895 he sold six or seven of his hives and gave the rest to his sister Bridget, who had since retained them as her property. The jury found both of the issues so raised in favour of the plaintiff.

Between the trial of the action and the hearing of the new trial motion the plaintiff died, and the action was revived in the name of his personal representative.

The following were the questions left to the jury and the answers:-

1. Were the injuries complained of caused by the bees having attacked and stung the mare and the plaintiff on the 20th September, 1900. *Answer - Yes*.

2. Were the said bees the property of Peter O'Gorman, Michael O'Gorman, or Bridget O'Gorman? *Answer* - Michael O'Gorman.

3. If of Michael O'Gorman, did he keep the bees on the land of the defendant Peter O'Gorman with his licence and permission? *Answer - Yes*

4. Were said bees kept on said lands negligently? *Answer* - Yes.

5. Were said bees kept on said lands in an unreasonable number, or at an unreasonable place, or with appreciable danger to the inhabitants of O'Gorman's adjoining farm? *Answer* - Yes.

6. Were said bees to the knowledge of the defendants, or either of them, and which of the defendants, of a dangerous and mischievous nature and accustomed to sting mankind or domestic animals? *Answer* - Yes, of both defendants.

7. Was the honey taken from the hive on the 20th September, 1900, with reasonable care, skill, and prudence? *Answer* - No.

8. Was the plaintiff guilty of the alleged negligence? *Answer* - No.

9. And if so, could the defendants by the exercise of ordinary care have avoided the consequences of plaintiff's negligence? *Answer* - Replay to No. 8 disposes of this.

10. Find damages? *Answer* - £200.

Upon these findings the learned Judge entered judgment for the plaintiff for £200 damages and costs.

The defendants moved to set aside the verdict and to have one entered for him on the grounds - (1) that the evidence disclosed no cause of action against the defendants or either of them; (2) that the evidence as to the numbers, place, and manner in which the bees were kept and in which the honey was taken on the 20th September, 1900, disclosed no case against the defendants either of actionable nuisance or actionable negligence, or of unreasonable or improper use of the lands; (3) that there was no evidence that the injuries to the plaintiff were caused by such alleged negligence or nuisance; (4) that the bees being animals "ferae naturae" over which the defendants had no control, the defendants were not liable for their acts outside the defendants' lands; (5) that the bees were not the property of either of the defendants; (6) that there was no evidence proper to be submitted to the jury in support of any of the issues left to them; (7) that the damage claimed for was too remote; and (8) that the learned Judge was in error in not acceding to the requisitions submitted on behalf of the defendants; or in the alternative for a new trial.

Matthew J.Bourke, K.C. (with him *Redmond Barry, K.C.,* and *Phelps*), for the defendants:-

Bee culture is an industry as old as the world itself, and never before has an action of this kind been instituted. Cases of liability for injury by ordinary domesticated animals afford no analogy. They rest on the principle that the owner of such animals is liable for injuries which are the natural result of allowing them to escape from his control. It is the same principle that governs the liability of parties who choose to bring any matter on their lands which may cause injury if it escapes. The cases of *Cox v. Burbidge* (13 C.B. (N.S.) 430) and *Fletcher v. Rylands* (L.R. 3 H.L.330) explain this principle and the limits of its application. It is on the same basis that the liability for wild animals which have been domesticated rests. Their owner by taking them into his keeping undertakes the duty of so controlling them as to prevent their doing mischief. If they escape from such control and do harm he is responsible (*Brady v. Warren* [1900] 2 I.R. 632). These considerations have no application to bees, whose nature and necessities of existence preclude all possibility of controlling them.

The impossibility of keeping certain animals under restraint, and the slightness of the damage ordinarily caused by them, are well recognised grounds of immunity in respect of them. In *Read v. Edwards* (17 C.B. (N.S.) 245 at p.260), Willes, J., notices the distinction between oxen and dogs or cats on account of the difficulty or impossibility of keeping the latter under restraint, secondly, the slightness of the damage which their wandering ordinarily causes, and thirdly, the common usage of mankind to allow them a wider liberty.

Once it is conceded that a man may keep bees, his right to keep something he cannot control is acknowledged, and leaves him free from liability for their unexpected or unusual fits of viciousness. At the trial of this case there was no evidence either direct or on cross-examination pointed at any specific negligence causing the injuries. The use of the veil in protection of the person removing the honey was the ordinary and invariable precaution on such occasions. It evidenced no consciousness of any particular danger to third parties. There was no evidence that the character of the hives used had anything to do with the occurrence. There was no evidence that the locality in which or the numbers in which the hives were kept constituted negligence in the defendants' mode of managing them, or occasioned or contributed to the injuries. In the absence of evidence to that effect there was nothing in this case but the fact that the defendants were owners of bees which stung the plaintiff's horse. In that state of things to hold the defendant liable would be to establish that the owner of one hive would be responsible for a sting inflicted by a single bee from that hive no matter how far from the locality of the hive.

The doctrine of scienter has no application. It is common knowledge that once a bee stings it loses its sting and dies.

Furthermore, the damage here is too remote. It was the result of the horse bolting and the plaintiff getting entangled in the reins. The occurrence was an accident upon an accident.

[The following cases were also referred to:- *Sanders v. Teape* (51 L.T. (N.S.) 263, *Brown v. Giles* (1 Car. & P. 118), *Lee v. Riley* (18 C.B. (N.S.) 722), *Osborne v. Chocqueel* [1896] 2 Q.B. 109; United States Digest - Title, Animals, 271]

The Solicitor-General (Campbell, K.C.) and *Bushe, K.C.* (with them *Lynch*), for the plaintiff:-

There was ample evidence to support the findings that the bees were kept in excessive numbers and too close to the plaintiffs farm. The defendant's appreciation of the dangerous nature of the operation he was about to engage in is proved by the precautions he took to protect himself. He was under an obligation to give his neighbours an opportunity of taking similar precautions or of getting beyond the reach of the bees, yet he gave no warning to the plaintiff or the other occupants of the adjoining farm.

Upon the authority of the United States decision scienter may be gathered from the fact that the animals causing the injury were of a ferocious species. There is no proof whatever that when a bee uses its sting it dies.

The damage is not too remote. A man is responsible who puts in motion a regular chain of events which finally cause the injury: *Scott v. Shepherd* (2 Wm. Bl. 893)

[The following cases were also referred to:- *Vaughan v. Menlove* 3 Bing. (N.S.) 468, *Smith v. London and South-Western Railway Company* L.R. 6 C.P. 14, *Lawrence v. Jenkins* L.R. 8 Q.B. 274, *Jones v. Boyce* 1 Stark. N.P. 493, *Byrne v. Great Southern and Western Railway Company* (Unreported), *Bell v. Great Northern Railway Company* 26 L.R. Ir. 428, *Clark v. Chambers* 3 Q.B.D. 327].

Barry, K.C. in reply.

KENNY, J.:-

We think we are in a position now, upon the very full argument we have heard in this case, to dispose of it without letting it stand for judgment. Upon the view we take, it has really been disposed of by the findings of the jury. The defendant's notice of motion asks that the verdict for the plaintiff may be set aside, and that a verdict be entered for the defendants on the grounds - [His Lordship read the grounds set forth in the notice of motion].

The case is an interesting and, to some extent, a novel one. The trial took place before Mr. Justice Johnson at the Spring Assizes of the present year, in the City of Limerick, with a special jury. The circumstances seem to have been very fully investigated, and the learned judge seems to have given the jury adequate instructions, and to have taken their opinion upon every material question. The trial resulted in a verdict for the plaintiff for the sum of £200.

The case is a sad one in this - that the plaintiff has died since the trial, in consequence, I cannot but infer, of the injuries sustained on the 20th September, 1900. It is manifest that he was telling the truth at the trial when he stated that he was unable to do a single day's work. The suit has been revived at the instance of his personal representative.

The statement of claim alleges that in September, 1900, and for some time previously, the defendants wrongfully, negligently, and injuriously kept on their lands a swarm, or swarms, of bees, well knowing that the said bees were of a dangerous and mischievous nature, and accustomed to sting mankind and domestic animals - that on the 20th September, 1900, the plaintiff was on his father's land, adjoining the defendants', doing his father's business, and having in his charge, and under his control, a horse the property of his father - that the bees swarmed on and attacked the plaintiff and the horse, and whilst the plaintiff was endeavouring to protect the horse, and to save and extricate himself from the swarm of bees, the plaintiff was severely stung and injured by the bees, and was knocked down and dragged along the ground, and struck against the wall by the horse, and sustained permanent injuries, and was permanently disabled. To that statement of claim every imaginable plea was put in, including one of contributory negligence. All I need say about the latter plea is that the jury very properly negatived any foundation for it.

The facts of the case are these. The plaintiff and the defendants are next door neighbours. The plaintiff and the defendant Peter O'Gorman are both small farmers in the county Clare, and for several years before the 20th September, 1900, the latter had collected, in a little field or garden on his own farm, but adjoining the plaintiff's house, a large number of beehives. The original number of hives was one, or two. The number then went up to six, and at the time that this unfortunate occurrence took place, on the 20th September, 1900, there were either twenty or twenty-two hives in this little garden. There was evidence that at various times, during the previous five years, complaints had been made of the bees having attacked men who were working on the plaintiff's farm. Even on the 20th September, 1900, a complaint was made in the earlier part of the day. Later on, the plaintiff was harnessing a horse in front of his own door. About four or five yards off was a little low fence of stone. While harnessing the horse the bees came across from the defendant's land and attacked both man and horse. It is not a question of an individual bee, or two or three bees. They must have come across in considerable numbers. The plaintiff was stung and the horse was frightened. The plaintiff had put the winkers on the horse, and just as he was putting on the collar the animal bolted, while the plaintiff held on to his head, or to some part of his body. The horse forced the plaintiff up against the stone fence and thus caused the injury to his spine, to which he ultimately succumbed. These incidents occurred almost in the space of a minute.

At the close of the case, the learned judge, having refused a direction, left the following questions to the jury, all of which were found in favour of the plaintiff - [His Lordship here read the questions and answers].

It would appear from the Judge's report than in connection with answer No. 5, with reference to the reasonable user of the land, the jury in reply to an interrogatory addressed to them stated that what they meant was that the bees were kept in unreasonable numbers, AND at an unreasonable place, *and* with appreciable danger to the inhabitants of plaintiff's farm.

The only questions that were argued before us were as to the reasonable user of the defendant's lands, and the remoteness of damage. It was conceded that bees were not *ferae naturae*, that the plaintiff's injuries were caused by his being forced up against the fence, and that the two defendants were to be regarded as owners of both the land and the bees. On the two questions submitted to us, we think that there was evidence fit to be submitted to the jury that the bees were kept in unreasonable numbers, and at an unreasonable place, and with appreciable danger to the occupiers of the plaintiff's farm, and, further, that the honey was not taken on the 20th September with reasonable care, skill, and prudence, and that the damages were not too remote. As to the first, it appears, as I have already said, that there had been complaints anterior to the 20th September, 1900. The complaints do not appear to have been frequent, but there was evidence that on occasions the plaintiff's men had to discontinue their work in the day time and come again in the evening when the bees had retired to their hives. On the morning of the 20th September complaints were made. The bees were all in the immediate vicinity of the plaintiff's house. The defendant Michael O'Gorman, who took the honey from the hives on that particular occasion, was armed *cap a pie*, and not only with offensive weapons, but with defensive armour. So far as he was concerned, not a single bee could do *him* the slightest harm. He proceeded to take the honey from one out of the twenty-two hives, all collected together in the same small enclosure. It might well be that the attempted destruction of one hive immediately adjacent to a number of others would have an irritating effect upon the occupants of the latter, and such a circumstance would be a material one for the jury in determining whether there had been want of care in taking the honey. But on the other issue as to the bees being kept in an unreasonable number or at an unreasonable place, or with appreciable danger to the inhabitants of the adjoining farm, there was evidence that the bees were kept within a few yards of the front of the plaintiff's dwelling-house, and in considerable numbers. It is not a question of one hive, or two, or three, but it is a question of at least twenty hives, kept in a small space in the immediate vicinity of the plaintiff's house.

I do not see how that evidence could have been withheld from the jury. The defendants were entitled to the natural and reasonable use of their own land, and the jury had to consider whether this keeping of bees in the manner and place in which they did, went beyond the lawful user of their own land in relation to their neighbour. It was a jury question, and there was, in my opinion, evidence upon which they could properly act. They found in effect that the defendant had set up what was an actionable nuisance, and that it resulted in injury to his neighbour. I do not think that that finding can be quarrelled with, and my opinion is supported by the dictum of Pollock, B., in *Farrer v. Nelson* 15 Q.B.D. 258, in which I concur. I therefore hold that the action lies.

As to remoteness of damage, I am of opinion that on this point also there is no reason for disturbing the verdict. The £200 have been awarded, not alone in respect of the injury which was caused to the plaintiff's spine, but also in respect of what he suffered directly from the stings of the bees. But assuming, as I think we reasonably may, that the greater portion of the sum has relation to the former, I do not think that the damage is too remote. The horse and man were both stung; the man was at the horse's head when the latter bolted up against the wall, crushing him against it. The whole occurrence was the work of a moment. The injury to the spine was not an incident that took place after an interval of time, but connected with and immediately following on the direct cause. Indeed the circumstances may be said to have been almost simultaneous.

The verdict and judgment for the plaintiff will therefore stand.

BARTON, J.:-

I have also come to the conclusion that this verdict ought not to be disturbed, but not without considerable hesitation. In the first place I do not think that the verdict can be supported by reference to the doctrine of "scienter" or "notice of mischievous propensities" of animals; or by reference to those cases in which defendants have been held liable for the "escape of animals" from their premises and control. These topics were adverted to in the course of the argument, but I hardly think that they were seriously pressed. In the next place, I doubt whether the verdict can be supported upon the ground of damage caused by nuisance or unreasonable user of land, or by reference to *Farrer v. Nelson* 15 Q.B.D. 258. That was a case of injury to crops from over stocking land with game - a user of land which was calculated to injure, and did injure, the crops. This is an action for personal injuries to a man, caused by a horse, which he was harnessing, being suddenly stung by bees. Mr. Barry argued that there was no evidence that the mere number and location of these hives was calculated to cause bees to sting the horse, or did cause the horse to be stung. Mr. Barry pointed out that plaintiff's injuries were caused by the use of the "smoker" which is an ordinary instrument of bee-keeping, always attended by some risk to persons in the immediate neighbourhood. That risk might be increased by the multiplication of hives; but he contended that the plaintiff's injuries were, upon the admitted facts of the case really attributable, not to a nuisance or to an unreasonable user of land, but to a particular act done on a particular occasion, namely, the smoking of the hives with this "smoker" when plaintiff happened to be near the hives.

If that be the true view of the case, it would seem to me that, if this verdict can be supported, it must be by reference to the facts and findings of the jury as to negligence. It is conceded that it was the defendant's operations with the "smoker" that caused the bees to sting the horse, and it cannot be doubted that a word of warning would have avoided all the harm. This is not denied, but defendant's counsel say that there was no duty and no liability, and that it was all a mere "accident upon an accident." Accordingly, we are met at the threshold of this branch of the case by the question - was any duty - such as our law will recognise - owed by defendant to plaintiff to warn him or otherwise take care while smoking these hives? In other words, Do the facts of this case bring it within those limited classes of case in which, in the absence of any contractual relation between the parties, a duty to be careful may be owed by one person to another? Upon this subject reference may be usefully made to some passages in the judgments delivered in the Court of Appeal in England in *Le Lievre v. Gould* [1893] 1 Q.B. 491 In that case Bowen, L.J., quoted with approval the judgment of Romer, J., in *Scholes v. Brook* 63 L.T. (N.S.) 837, in which the learned Judge divided the cases, in which a duty to take care may arise apart from contract, into two classes, viz., those falling under the doctrine of "invitation to premises" and those arising out of the careless using, managing, or dealing with dangerous instruments or things. With reference to the latter class, Bowen, L.J., said, at p. 502:- "Take, for example, the case of the owner of a chattel, such as a horse, a gun, or a carriage, *or any other instrument*, which is in itself of such a character that, if it be used carelessly, it may injure some third person who is near to it, then it is as plain as daylight that the owner of that chattel, who is responsible for its management, is bound to be careful how he uses it." Lord Esher, M.R., at p.497, said:- "If one man is near to another, or is near to the property of another, a duty lies upon him not to do that which may cause a personal injury to that other, or may injure his property." A.L.Smith, L.J., at p.504, adopted the rule that "a duty to take care did arise when the person or property of one was in such proximity to the person or property of another that, if due care was not taken, damage might be done by the one to the other." These are *dicta* of high authority; and it becomes necessary to consider whether they have not some application to the facts of the present case.

This case certainly cannot be represented as a mere case of a man who has been injured in consequence of a sting from a neighbour's bee. If that was all, there could be no duty and no liability. The facts of the case are special and unusual, and Mr. Bushe argued that there was evidence that defendant, when proceeding to smoke these hives, knew, or ought to have known, that his neighbour was likely to be at that very time - as in fact he was - in immediate proximity to the hives tackling his horse. Plaintiff's witnesses gave evidence to that effect, and defendant made significant admissions in the same direction. It was proved that this was the usual time for plaintiff to come to this spot for the purpose of tackling his horse, and defendant's knowledge that the horse was at this spot close to the hives at the time, and that it was plaintiff's habit to tackle there, was admitted. For example, I find that defendant said in cross-examination - "I saw the horse in the yard feeding there and before. They were in the habit of bringing the horse there at dinner time, and to tackle there." It was also pointed out that it appeared from his admissions in cross-examination that he was a farmer and bee-keeper acquainted with the ways of bees and of horses, and with the serious consequences of bees stinging horses. Apparently it was on account of risks and inconveniences of that kind that he located his twenty-two hives at some distance from his own stables and yard. It had been brought definitely to defendant's notice by complaints that his neighbours had been forced, on account of the bees to cease working on several occasions in the neighbourhood of the hives. Risk of injury from smoking the hives might be increased by the collection of so many hives in a small space. It is clear that defendant knew that the operation of applying the "smoker" to the hives was attended by some danger of physical injury to any person in the immediate neighbourhood. The best possible evidence of this was afforded by the ample precautions which he thought it prudent to adopt for his own safety. He wore a crape veil. His hands were covered, and he was enveloped in a cloak. As he said, "I had a proper dress on". Mr. Bourke truly said that this is a usual precaution for a bee-keeper to adopt when smoking hives. That is so; but it only shows that a "smoker" is an instrument which, when applied to beehives, is, to apply Bowen,L.J.'s *dictum*, of such a character that it may cause injury to a person who is near, unless some precaution be taken.

Under these circumstances, was it unreasonable or contrary to law for the jury to come to the conclusion that there was - having regard especially to the knowledge which he possessed of the likelihood that plaintiff would be harnessing his horse in immediate proximity to the hives, and to the precautions which he adopted for his own safety - some duty cast upon defendant towards his neighbour to warn him or take some other precaution? Mr. Barry truly said that bee-keeping is an ancient and useful industry. But if the handling of an instrument or the carrying out of an operation connected with an industry, however ancient and useful, is, under special circumstances, such as were given in evidence and found by the jury in this case, attended by danger of physical injury to a person in the immediate neighbourhood, and if the person using the instrument or carrying out the operation has or ought to have knowledge of that danger to that person - in such a case may not a duty arise towards that person to take care, the breach of which may result in actionable negligence? Would not a duty to take care arise in the case of a man blasting rocks or felling trees at his boundary fence with knowledge that within the ambit of the fall of rocks or trees it might reasonably be anticipated that his neighbour would be tackling his horse? Cases of that kind may differ from the present case in degree of danger and of gravity; but in principle is there not a resemblance?

It has not been brought to our notice that there was any misdirection by the learned Judge at the trial on the subject of remoteness of damage. If it be the correct view of this case that the jury were entitled to say that defendant ought to have anticipated risk of the kind of harm which happened to plaintiff, and ought to have warned him or taken some other precaution on his account, then it can hardly be disputed that all that befell plaintiff flowed naturally from the negligence of defendant. It is a case in which effect followed cause with great rapidity - in fact almost instantaneously. There was no intervening act of any third party. The tripping in the reins was caused by the horse turning when stung. The holding to the reins was not an unreasonable thing for plaintiff to do in the peril which defendant's negligence had placed him. Defendant's counsel seemed to me, upon the question of remoteness of damage, to be driven to contend that, even if it be conceded that that there was evidence of an act negligently performed and of damage flowing directly therefrom, the defendant ought not to be held responsible for consequences so much greater than could have been reasonable anticipated by him. But, as Blackburn J., said in *Smith v. London and South-Western Railway Company* L.R. 6 C.P. 14, at p. 21, "What the defendants might reasonably anticipate is only material with reference to the question whether the defendants were negligent or not, and cannot alter their liability if they were guilty of negligence." Once negligence is established, it is no answer that the damage, if it followed in the natural course of things, was more serious than was or might have been expected. Much mischief may flow, in a few seconds of time, as the natural consequences of a comparatively trivial form of negligence.

The case is, in my opinion, by no means free from difficulty, and I have arrived at the conclusion that the verdict ought not to be disturbed after much hesitation. My doubt, in the course of the argument, has specially had reference to the question whether the danger of the kind of harm which happened to plaintiff was sufficiently obvious to be such a danger as defendant could be legally bound to observe and avoid. But, on the whole, I do not feel disposed to dissent from the view that there was evidence for the jury upon the subject. If that be so, it would be an invasions of their province to interfere with their verdict. I have also felt hesitation because, in one respect, the case is a novel one from the point of view of legal liability. I am not aware of any other case in which liability for personal injuries caused by a frightened horse has been maintained where the cause of the horse's fright was stinging by bees. But in cases of high authority defendants have been held liable for personal injuries inflicted on a plaintiff by a horse frightened by some unexpected impact, or sight, or noise, the result of nuisance or of negligence. It is difficult to imagine anything more calculated to terrify a horse, and to result in injury to a man engaged in harnessing the horse, than sudden stinging by bees. If terror of that kind, followed by injury to plaintiff, is directly traceable to the negligent act of a defendant, why should he escape liability?

For these reasons I do not feel prepared to say that the jury could not reasonably come to the conclusion that the plaintiff's injuries were directly attributable to the defendant's negligence.

WRIGHT, J., concurred, holding that the doctrine of *scienter* did not apply, and that the case was disposed of by the findings of the jury, more particularly by their answer to the fifth question submitted to them.

Solicitor for the plaintiff: *F.F.Cullinan.*
Solicitor for the defendants: *James B. Molony.*

J.L.

III   **1906. Canada.**
                                                LUCAS v. PETTIT
Editors' Introductory Notes

Mulock,C.J. said that the doctrine of *scienter* or "notice of mischievous propensities" had no application to that case, nor could the absence of negligence, in the sense pressed upon him relieve the defendant of liability.
That the bees because of their numbers and position on the defendant's land, were

dangerous to the plaintiff, and also that the defendant had reason so to believe. It was the defendant's right to have on his premises a reasonable number of bees, or bees so placed as not to unfairly interfere with the rights of his neighbour.

REPORT
Of
LUCAS v. PETTIT
(1906) XII ONTARIO LAW REPORTS 448
D.C. 1906, Sept.24.

Animals-Escape of Bees-Injury to Neighbour-Negligence-Scienter-Danger from Number and situation of Bees-Findings of Jury.

The defendant placed a large number of hives of bees upon his own land within 100 feet of the plaintiff's land. While the plaintiff was at work with two horses upon his own land the bees attacked and stung the horses so that they died, and also stung and injured the plaintiff. In an action to recover damages for his loss and injury, the jury found, *inter alia*, that the bees were in ordinary flight at the time of the occurrence; that they were the defendant's bees; and that the defendant had reasonable grounds for believing that his bees were, by reason of the situation of his hives, or their numbers, dangerous to persons or horses upon the highway or elsewhere than on the defendant's premises:-

Held, that the doctrine of *scienter*, or notice of mischievous propensities of the bees, had no application, nor could the absence of negligence, other than as found by the jury, relieve the defendant; it was his right to have on his premises a reasonable number of bees, or bees so placed as not unfairly to interfere with the rights of his neighbour, but if the number was reasonable, or if they were so placed as to interfere with his neighbour in the fair enjoyment of his rights, then what would otherwise have been lawful became an unlawful act; the finding of the jury meant that the bees, because of their number and situation, were dangerous to the plaintiff; and the defendant was liable for the injury flowing directly from his unlawful act.

Judgment of Magee, J., affirmed.

MOTION of behalf of the defendant to set aside the findings of the jury at the trial, and the judgment of Magee, J., entered thereon, and to enter judgment for the defendant.

The following statement of the facts is taken from the judgment of Mulock, C.J.Ex.D.:-

The action was brought for injuries caused by bees of the defendant, under the following circumstances.

The defendant was the owner of 160 or 170 hives of bees, which he placed in a small yard situate within some 20 feet of the highway running east and west. At the southerly end of this yard was a small building with a frontage of about 24 feet on the highway, and being about 18 feet in depth and 17 feet in height. From north to south, the yard occupied by the hives was about 124 feet in length. Immediately opposite this yard on the south side of the road was the plaintiff's property, consisting of a field of about 8 acres, which was in oats, and beyond it another field in buckwheat. The highway is about 56 feet in width. On the 10th August, 1905, the plaintiff proceeded to the oat field with a pair of horses and a binder for the purpose of cutting the oats, when the horses were attacked by a large number of bees. The horses ran away from the plaintiff, dragging the binder with them to the south end of the field, and there stopped at the fence. The plaintiff followed them and endeavoured to unhitch and take them away, but was unable to make them move. He himself was being similarly attacked, and made his escape by immersing himself in a neighbouring pool of water and covering the exposed portions of his body with mud. One of the horses died almost at once in the field from the effect of the stings, and the other succumbed within two or three days. The plaintiff himself suffered severely, and was under medical treatment.

The questions put to the jury and their answers are as follows:-

1. Were the plaintiff, Lucas, and his horses injured by bees engaged in ordinary flight or work or by the swarming of a colony of bees? A. Ordinary flight.

2. If they were injured by bees engaged in ordinary work and flight, were those the defendant's bees? A. Yes

3. If the plaintiff and his horses were injured by the swarming of a colony of bees, had the bees swarmed from the defendant's colony? No answer.

4. Had the defendant reasonable grounds for believing that his bees were more dangerous than ordinary bees? A. Yes

5. Had the defendant reasonable grounds for believing that his bees were, by reason of the situation of his hives, or their numbers, dangerous to persons or horses upon the highway or elsewhere than on the defendant's premises? A. Yes

6. At what sum do you assess the damages of the plaintiff, if the defendant be liable for damages? A. $400

On these findings the learned trial Judge entered a judgment for the plaintiff for $400, and from that judgment the defendant appeals.

The appeal was hear by a Divisional Court composed of MULOCK, C.J.Ex.D., ANGLIN and CLUTE, JJ., on the 17th September, 1906.

G.Lynch-Staunton, K.C., for the defendant. On the answers of the jury judgment should not have been entered for the plaintiff, and there was no case to go to the jury. It was not proved that the bees which attacked the plaintiff were the defendant's bees. They may just as probably have been the bees of Misener, another neighbour. The defendant had 160 hives of bees, and Misener had only 6 or 7, but he had enough to kill the horses. The fact that the defendant had more bees did not warrant the finding. The defendant's bees had been carried there a few days before the injury to the plaintiff. The bee is a harmless domesticated animal, not prone to attack man. Even if the bees were the defendant's is he liable? What duty did he owe? Is the owner of bees in the same position as the owner of a lion or tiger? If not, *scienter* must be established by the person complaining, as in the case of a dog. Bee culture is lawful: *Earl v. Van Alstine* (1850), 8 Barb. 630. It is not a question for the jury whether bees are domestic or wild animals. There was no evidence to go to the jury that they are wild animals. The next question is as to danger from the situation of the hives. *O'Gorman v. O'Gorman*, [1903] 2 I.R. 573, was relied on by the plaintiff, but see *Le Lievre v. Gould*, [1893] 1 Q.B. 491. The bee is a free commoner, and can go and come. He is useful and not ferocious. If a man is liable for keeping bees, the honey industry will be stopped. The evidence is that the situation of the hives near the highway was not dangerous. The jury found that they were not swarming. They do not swarm at the owner's risk. Mere location and number is not evidence of negligence. There is no evidence upon which the defendant can be held liable.

W. S. McBrayne, for the plaintiff. Bees are *ferae naturae*: Blackstone, Lewis's Am. ed., book 2, ch. 25, p. 390; they are not domesticated, but may be cultivated: *Parsons v. Manser* (1903), 62 L.R.A. 132, and notes. As to *scienter*, there can be no question if the bees are in a wild state — the owner harbours wild animals at his own risk. Notice of vicious propensities is not required. The owner of an animal not shewn to be harmless by nature or cultivation, takes the risk: *Filburn v. People's Palace and*

Aquarium Co. (1890), 25 Q.B.D. 258; Ingham's Law of Animals, p. 391. A man is, at any rate, liable for damages if his animal trespasses on another's property: *Patterson v. Fanning* (1901), 2 O.L.R. 462; *Cox v. Burbridge* (1863), 13 C.B.N.S. 430.

Lynch-Staunton, in reply, referred to the *Filburn* case, *supra* at p. 260; Lee v. Riley (1865), 18 C.B.N.S. 722; *Read v. Edwards* (1864), 17 C.B.N.S. 245, 260.

September 24. The judgment of the court was delivered by Mulock, C.J. (after setting out the facts as above): - There is abundance of evidence, I think, to support the findings of the jury (except the answer to question No 4, which is not material to the issue), and the question is, whether they warrant the judgment in question.

It was estimated that the strength of a hive was between 15,000 and 50,000 bees, and the plaintiff speaks of them as attacking the horses and himself in clouds. He estimated that there were more than four bushels of bees on the horses and in the air. This, of course, is a mere estimate, but it is clear that the number of the defendant's bees was very great.

For the defence it was contended that the defendant was guilty of no negligence, and that there was no evidence that the bees were of a vicious nature, and that the defendant was not aware of any viciousness or propensity on the part of the bees to attack mankind or animals.

The doctrine of *scienter* or "notice of mischievous propensities" of the bees has, I think, no application to this case, nor could the absence of negligence, in the sense pressed upon us, relieve the defendant of liability.

The facts shew that the defendant placed a very large number of hives of bees within 100 feet of the plaintiff's land, and that in the course of their ordinary flight between the hives and the plaintiff's field of buckwheat they would pass directly over the plaintiff's intervening field of oats, where it was necessary for the plaintiff to be for the purpose of harvesting the same.

The right of a person to enjoy and deal with his own property as he chooses is controlled by his duty to so use it as not to affect injuriously the rights of others, and in this case it is a pure question of fact whether the defendant collected on his land such an unreasonably large number of bees or placed them in such position thereon as to interfere with the reasonable enjoyment of the plaintiff's land. I think the reasonable deduction from the answer of the jury to question 5 is that the bees, because of their numbers and position on the defendant's land, were dangerous to the plaintiff, and also that the defendant had reason so to believe. In my view it is immaterial whether or not the defendant, under these circumstances, regarded the bees as dangerous. If he was making an unreasonable use of his premises, and injury resulted therefrom to the plaintiff, he is liable.

It was the defendant's right to have on his premises a reasonable number of bees, or bees so placed as not to unfairly interfere with the rights of his neighbour, but if the number was unreasonable, or if they were so placed as to interfere with his neighbour in the fair enjoyment of his rights, then what would otherwise have been lawful, becomes an unlawful act. In this case the jury found as a matter of fact that the bees, because of their number and situation, were dangerous to the plaintiff. The defendant was acting unlawfully, and he is liable for the injury flowing directly from such unlawful act: *O'Gorman v. O'Gorman*, [1903] 2 I.R. 573; *Farrer v. Nelson* (1885) 15 Q.B.D. 258,260.

The appeal should be dismissed with costs.

E.B.B.

IV   **1906. England.**
PARKER v. REYNOLDS
Editors' Introductory Notes.

This is an extremely valuable report as it is one of the few High Court Cases we have on the subject. It is unfortunate that it is so brief. The Judge, the plaintiff and the defendant were all beekeepers so that they would understand the subject of beekeeping. The Judge's decision has become a classic of its kind and sets out the principles simply and clearly.

Mr. Justice Phillimore said in his judgment that if the Jury thought that the plaintiff could not live at home in the ordinary way in August according to the simple English ideas, and that his reasonable comfort was substantially interfered with owing to the defendant's bees, they might come to the conclusion that there was a nuisance.

REPORT
Of
PARKER v. REYNOLDS
The Times Monday 17th December 1906 Page 12
THE ASSIZES
MIDLAND CIRCUIT

At Birmingham, last Thursday, before Mr. Justice Phillimore and a common jury, the hearing of Parker v. Reynolds was concluded.

Mr. Hugo Young K.C. and Mr. J.G.Hurst appeared for the plaintiff; Mr. Maddocks was for the defendant.

The plaintiff and the defendant were neighbours and fellow-members of the Bee Keepers' Association. The plaintiff asked for an injunction against the defendant to restrain him from continuing a nuisance. The defendant kept ten hives of bees in his garden and placed them against a fence which was common to both the plaintiff and the defendant, and within about 20ft. of the plaintiff's house. These hives accommodated about half a million bees, and in the summer of 1905 these bees, according to the plaintiff, invaded his house to such an extent as to be a nuisance, and stung his wife, children and servants. The plaintiff kept his bees about 200 yards away in a field. The defendant pleaded that no nuisance was caused by his bees.

Various experts were called, who gave evidence as to the habits of bees.

MR. JUSTICE PHILLIMORE, in summing up, said this kind of action was a most unusual one. The allegation was that the plaintiff could not lead his ordinary life or eat his ordinary food without his household being in danger of constant stinging, so large a number of bees coming into the house. After reviewing the evidence, his Lordship said that if they thought that the plaintiff could not live at home in the ordinary way in August according to the simple English ideas, and that his reasonable comfort was substantially interfered with owing to the defendant's bees, they might come to the conclusion that there was a nuisance.

The Jury found that the presence of the bees constituted a nuisance, and recommended that the hives be removed to a spot some 200 yards away. An injunction was granted to the plaintiff against the defendant, with costs. Stay of execution was granted on the usual undertakings.

V   1931. New Zealand
ROBINS v. KENNEDY AND COLUMB
Editors' Introductory Notes.

The magistrate founded his original judgment both on negligence and on the Rule in *Rylands v. Fletcher* (the reference to water) and the *scienter* doctrine (the reference to wild and dangerous animals). The appeal judge decided that the real cause of action was negligence which meant that he did not have to decide the other points but it seems clear that he was not very impressed with them. The maxim *sic utere tuout alienum non laedas* sets out the principle of neighbourliness -" so to use your own property that you do not harm another". *Cur. adv. vult.* is short for *curia advisari vult* - "the court wishes to be advised" - and means that the judgment was reserved and given at a later date. A court is said to "take judicial notice" of something that is so well known that it does not need further proof. It is heartening for beekeepers that the court was not prepared to take judicial notice of the vicious habits of bees.

Bees kept in unreasonable numbers and at an unreasonable place and with appreciable danger to a neighbour, having done damage, were held to affect their owner with liability.

Probably the keeping of a few ordinary hives in an ordinary place would not render the owner liable for damages for their stings, in the absence of negligence.

The appellant was guilty of negligence in keeping so many hives of bees on the boundary of Kennedy's land, and this negligence was the effective cause of the injury and damage

The American authors to whom the judge had access considered there was no liability apart from negligence.

REPORT
Of
ROBINS v. KENNEDY and COLUMB
[1931] N.Z. L.R. 1134.
S.C. IN BANCO. CHRISTCHURCH. 1931 August 4; October 1. ADAMS, J.

Negligence-Negligent keeping of Bees-Bees kept in Unreasonable Numbers and at an Unreasonable Place-Whether Liability absolute-Bees not in Category of Dangerous Animals-Registered Apiary-Registration not exempting Apiarist from Common-law Liability-Apiaries Act, 1927.

The appellant kept about seventy hives of bees on a small piece of land adjoining the respondent Kennedy's farm. While the respondents were reaping close to the apiary, bees in great numbers attacked the respondents and their horses, causing serious injuries. In an action for damages, the learned Magistrate found as a fact that the appellant (defendant) was guilty of negligence; and further, apart from negligence, the liability of a beekeeper was coextensive with the liability of a person keeping on his land water, wild and dangerous animals or poisonous fumes. From this judgment the defendant appealed.

Held (dismissing the appeal),

1. That the Apiaries Act, 1927, being restrictive and not permissive does not exempt a registered apiarist from common-law liability for injuries inflicted by his bees.

Frew and McCrostie v. Stewart [1928] N.Z.L.R. 806; G.L.R. 252 applied

Vaughan v. Taff Vale Railway Co. [1860] 5 H.&N. 679 distinguished

2. That the appellant was guilty of negligence in keeping so many hives of bees on the boundary, and that this negligence was the effective cause of the injury and damage.

O'Gorman v. O'Gorman [1903] 2 Ir. R. 573 followed.

3. The court will not take judicial notice of the vicious habits of bees.

Manton v. Brocklebank [1923] 2 K.B. 212 applied.

Quaere, Whether bees can be placed in the category of dangerous animals.

Appeal from the decision of a Magistrate awarding damages to respondents for injuries inflicted by bees.

The following facts are taken from the judgment of Adams, J.: The appellant kept about seventy hives, containing some millions of bees, on a small area of land on the boundary of part of the respondent Kennedy's farm. On the 25th February, while the respondents were reaping a crop of oats close to the apiary, bees in great numbers attacked Kennedy's horses, stinging them so severely that two died and another was seriously injured, while both respondents were incapacitated for several days. In an action for damages, the learned Magistrate found as a fact that the appellant was guilty of negligence in keeping his bees in unreasonable numbers and at an unreasonable place, and with appreciable danger to the inhabitants of and others lawfully resorting to the adjoining farm; and, that apart from negligence, the liability of a beekeeper was coextensive with the liability of a person keeping on his land water or wild and dangerous animals.

Rolleston for the appellant.

Campbell for the respondents.

Rolleston:-

The Magistrate's judgment is based on (a) absolute liability, following the doctrine laid down in *Rylands v. Fletcher* L.R. 3 H.L. 330; (b) negligence in the manner of keeping the bees. The doctrine of absolute liability does not apply to animals which it is impossible to control: *O'Gorman v. O'Gorman* [1903] 2 Ir. R. 573. This case also shows that bees are not ferae naturae: see also *Halsbury* Vol 1, p. 375. The Legislature has by various Apiaries Acts encouraged the bee industry: See Apiaries Act, 1906, long title, and also the Honey-export Control Act, 1924. The finding of negligence is not justified, and this court is free to draw its own inferences on this head: *Grace v. Hannah* [1919] N.Z. L.R. 481; G.L.R. 421. The appellant's apiary was licensed under the Apiaries Act, the form of application for the license making it necessary to state (a) the location of the apiary, (b) the number of hives, and (c) the quality of the bees. There was no act of negligence on the part of the appellant, he being many miles away from the apiary at the time of the occurrence. The respondent was the author of his own trouble by unnecessarily provoking the bees in the heat of a summer day. As the appellant had a statutory authority for the position of his apiary and the position of his hives, there can be no liability: *Vaughan v. Taff Vale Railway Co.* [1860] 5 H. & N. 679. The only negligence that can be charged against the appellant is that he is an apiarist, an industry which the law encourages. All the Magistrate's findings of fact are referable not to any specific act of negligence on the part of the appellant, but to the fact that he is an apiarist. The number of bees is not material, because it has not been shown that the damage could not have happened had there been only one hive.

Campbell:-

The appellant's apiary, placed alongside the boundary of Kennedy's land, contained seventy hives, holding three to four million bees, which were in fact and to the knowledge of the appellant dangerous to persons and animals using Kennedy's paddock during the sunny hours of the day. These bees admittedly caused the damage complained of. As to negligence, there was ample evidence justifying the Magistrate's finding of negligence. The bees were kept in unreasonable numbers, at an unreasonable place, and to the danger of people on the adjoining property. This evidence could not have been withdrawn from a jury, and justified the

Magistrate, sitting as a jury, in finding negligence: *O'Gorman v. O'Gorman* [1903] 2 Ir.R. 573, per Kenny, J. *ibid* 581, 582, and per Wright, J. *ibid* 588. Barton, J., unlike Kenny and Wright, JJ., who relied on the unreasonable numbers, position, and dangerous character of the bees, seems to rely on the use of a "smoking" instrument; but he cites authorities to show that the principle he was applying as to the breach by defendant of a duty towards plaintiffs to take care by warning them or taking some other precaution applies also to the management of bees. Also, the defendant infringed the rule contained in the maxim, *sic utere tuo ut alienum non laedas*.

This seems to be the *ratio decidendi* of the Canadian case *Tellier v. Pelland* 2 E.& E. Digest p. 237. It is stated to be the *ratio decidendi* of another Canadian case, *Lucas v. Pettit* 2 E.& E. Digest p. 237. It may not be necessary to go so far as to say that there is an absolute liability on beekeepers for any damage done by their bees, on the principle of other dangerous agencies, such as wild animals, because it seems doubtful whether bees are animals of wild nature, although , as the Magistrate's judgment shows it is common knowledge that they sting human beings and horses in daytime. The reference in *Halsbury* Vol. 1, p. 377, par. 821, and p. 375 par. 817, seems doubtful on this point whether bees, as a matter of law, are of savage nature, but it is clear that one who keeps a tame animal with knowledge that it has in fact a dangerous propensity is liable for the animal's exercise of that propensity: *May v. Burdett* 72 R.R. 189,196; *Cox v. Burbidge* 134 R.R. 586,589,591, per Erle, C.J., and per Willes, J.; *Manton v. Brocklebank [1923]* 2 K.B. 212,226,230, per Warrington, L.J., and per Atkin, L.J.; *Paterson v. Fleming* 23 N.Z. L.R. 676, 704, 713, per Williams, J., and per Cooper and Chapman, JJ. Therefore the keeper of even a tame animal with a dangerous propensity is, as regards the animal's exercise of that propensity, in the same position as the keeper of a wild animal, and to that extent is subject to the rule of absolute liability laid down in *Rylands v. Fletcher* [1868] L.R. 3 H.L. 330. The rule in *Rylands v. Fletcher* applies to cases where by an excessive use of some private right a person has exposed his neighbour's property or person to danger. In such a case should accident happen therefrom, even through the intervention of an event for which he is not responsible and without negligence on his part, he is liable for the damage: *Wing v. London General Omnibus Co.* [1909] 2 K.B. 652, 665, per Fletcher Moulton, L.J. The keeping of bees in excessive numbers, thereby causing substantial inconvenience to another, is a nuisance, and may be restrained by injunction: *Parker v. Reynolds* 2 E.& E.. Digest p. 252, par. 341. When a nuisance is created, the author of the nuisance is liable to pay for all damage occasioned thereby to any member of the public, even though nobody has chosen to seek by injunction the complete remedy of stopping the nuisance: *Wing v. London General Omnibus Co.* [1909] 2 K.B. 652, 666, per Fletcher Moulton, L.J. The creation of a nuisance is a disregard of the *sic utere* rule. As to this maxim, see *Halsbury* Vol. 21, pp. 524 to 530, paras. 881, 888, 889, 896. As to the Apiaries Act, this is not enabling, but restrictive of an old existing right to keep bees, and therefore does not affect the common-law liability of a beekeeper: *Frew and McCrostie v. Stewart* [1928] G.L.R. 252

Cur. adv. vult.

Adams, J.:-

This is an appeal on law and fact from a judgment of the Magistrate's court at Timaru.

[After setting out the facts, His Honour continued:] The appellant contends, in the first place, that his apiary being registered under the Apiaries Act, 1927, he is authorised by statute to carry on his business and to keep bees for that purpose, and is therefore not under any duty to prevent injury or damage to his neighbour such as has been suffered by the respondents. For this proposition Mr. Rolleston relies on the principle established in *Vaughan v. Taff Vale Railway Co.*[1860] 5 H.& N.679. In that case the railway company was expressly authorized by the statute 8 & 9 Vict., c.20, s. 86 to use and employ locomotive and other engines in its business, and the use of fire to generate steam in the locomotive boiler was essential to the running of its trains. It was therefore held that the company was not liable for damages caused by a fire originated by sparks from the locomotive, there being no negligence. The principle established in *Vaughan v. Taff Vale Railway Co.* is stated by Cockburn, C.J., in the following passage from his judgment: "Although it may be true that if a person keeps an animal of known dangerous propensities, or a dangerous instrument, he will be responsible to those who are thereby injured, independently of any negligence in the mode of dealing with the animal or using the instrument; yet when the legislature has sanctioned and authorised the use of a particular thing, and it is used for the purpose for which it was authorised, and every precaution has been observed to prevent injury, the sanction of the legislature carries with it this consequence, that if damage results from the use of such thing independently of negligence, the party using it is not responsible."

The Apiaries Act, 1906, was the first statute passed in this country to regulate the bee industry. The long title of that Act was "An Act to encourage and protect the Bee Industry in New Zealand," and this title also appears in the Act passed in the following year, but was omitted in the consolidated Act of 1908 and does not appear in the present Act. In all these acts, however, the object plainly is to improve the yield and quality of the honey, and to encourage the industry by raising the quality and so increasing the demand, and this object is obtained by the strict observance of the conditions imposed. The Act, however, is not permissive, but restrictive. There is, therefore, no analogy between this case and *Vaughan's case*. It is true that the Act requires every person keeping bees to obtain a certificate from an inspector; but this is no more than a certificate that the apiarist has complied with the provisions of the Act, without which he is not permitted to carry on his business. In this connection Mr Campbell cited *Frew and McCrostie v. Stewart* [1928] N.Z. L.R. 806 in which I had occasion to consider a similar submission made by the appellants in relation to the provisions of the Motor-vehicles Act, 1924.

The learned Magistrate has found as a fact that the appellant was guilty of negligence, and also held that, apart from negligence, the liability of a beekeeper is coextensive with the liability of a person keeping on his land water, wild and dangerous animals, or poisonous fumes.

I shall first consider the question of liability on the ground of negligence. The facts as stated in the case are not disputed, but counsel for the appellant submits that the Magistrate has relied on common knowledge in the passage of his judgment: "It is common knowledge, of course, that bees when in large numbers are apt to suddenly and viciously attack human beings and horses during the heat of a summer day."

A similar objection was considered by Lord Sterndale in *Manton v. Brocklebank* [1923] 2 K.B. 212. In that case the Deputy County Court Judge held that as a consequence of its being natural to all horses when turned into a field with other horses to kick and bite in play as well as in quarrel, they are dangerous animals, and this was not supported by proper evidence. Lord Sterndale says *ibid.* 221: "The learned Deputy County Court Judge, however, refers to *Lee v. Riley* 18 C.B. (N.S.) 722 as supporting that proposition. I do not see that any such statement of fact was made by any of the judges who decided that case. What they decided was that if the defendant's horse was trespassing, and so giving a cause of action to the plaintiff, the act of the horse in kicking another was not so alien to horse nature as to make the resulting damage too remote to be recovered. This was also the decision in *Ellis v. Loftus Iron Co.L.R.* 10 C.P. 10, and neither of these cases seems to me to establish the proposition of fact stated by the Deputy County Court Judge. I assume however. that he acted, as did Darling and Salter, JJ., upon common knowledge of which the court must take notice. With respect, I think this is rather dangerous. There may be facts of such public notoriety that a court is bound to take notice of them, but the experience of different judges may well lead them to different conclusions as to the habits of horses, and I do not rely on any experience of my own." I think that in such cases there should be evidence to support the finding of fact.

In *O'Gorman v. O'Gorman* [1903] 2 Ir. R. 573 the plaintiff and the defendant resided on adjacent farms. The defendant, who was a farmer acquainted with the ways and management of bees and horses, placed about twenty hives of bees at the boundary- fence between the two farms. The defendant, for the purpose of getting honey, "smoked" the hives. The bees. irritated by the smoke swarmed upon the plaintiff and his horse. There was evidence that the plaintiff was likely to be "tackling" his horse at the place, but he did not warn the plaintiff or take precautions. The bees swarmed on the plaintiff and his horse, and inflicted severe injuries. A jury found that the bees were kept negligently in unreasonable numbers, and at an unreasonable place, with appreciable danger to the inhabitants of the plaintiff's farm. On these findings the trial Judge entered judgment for the plaintiff, and the case came before the King's Bench Division (Ireland) on a motion to set aside the judgment and enter judgment for the defendant. The motion was dismissed. Kenny, J., was of the opinion that there was evidence fit to be submitted to the jury that the bees were kept in unreasonable numbers, and at an unreasonable place, and with appreciable danger to the occupiers of the plaintiff's farm; and, further, that the honey was not taken with reasonable care, and there was evidence that the bees were kept within a few yards of the plaintiff's dwellinghouse and in considerable numbers. He said that the jury found, in effect, that the defendant had set up what was an actionable nuisance, and that it resulted in injury to his neighbour. I do not think that finding can be quarrelled with. Barton, J., was unable to support the verdict by reference to the doctrine of *scienter* or notice of mischievous propensities of animals, or by reference to cases of escape of animals from their premises or control, or on the ground of nuisance or unreasonable use of land. His judgment is founded on negligence, adopting the observations of Bowen, L.J., and Smith L.J., in *Le Lievre v. Gould* [1893] 1 Q.B. 491,497,504. Wright, J., concurred, holding that the doctrine of *scienter* did not apply, and that the case was disposed of by the findings of the jury - more particularly by their answer to the fifth question. The findings of the jury were as follows:-

"1. The injuries complained of were caused by the bees having attacked and stung the mare and the plaintiff on the 20th September, 1900.

"2. The bees were the property of Michael O'Gorman.

"3. Michael O'Gorman kept the bees on the land of the defendant Peter O'Gorman with his license and permission.

"4. The bees were kept on the said premises negligently.

"5. The bees were kept on the said lands in an unreasonable number, at an unreasonable place, and with appreciable danger to the inhabitants of O'Gorman's adjoining farm.

"6. The bees were, to the knowledge of both defendants, of a dangerous and mischievous nature, and accustomed to sting mankind and domestic animals.

"7. The honey was not taken from the hives on the 20th September, 1900, with reasonable care, skill and prudence.

"8. The plaintiff was not guilty of the alleged negligence."

O'Gorman's case [1903] 2 Ir. R. 573 is referred to in *Bevan on Negligence* 4th ed. (1928), Vol. 1, p. 666, note (k). The note reads: "Bees kept in unreasonable numbers and at an unreasonable place and with appreciable danger to a neighbour, having done damage, were held to affect their owner with liability." It is also cited in *Halsbury's Laws of England* Vol. 1, p. 375, note (p) where it is said that probably the keeping of a few ordinary hives in an ordinary place would not render the owner liable for damages by their stings, in the absence of negligence, and in Vol. 21, p. 379, and also in *Salmond on Torts* 7th ed. by Stallibrass, p. 352, continuation of note (m), at p. 351. Neither the industry of counsel nor my own search have discovered any adverse criticism of this case. I think, in the circumstances, the appellant was guilty of negligence in keeping so many hives of bees on the boundary of Kennedy's land, and that this negligence was the effective cause of the injury and damage.

It is therefore, unnecessary to determine whether there is liability in such cases without proof of negligence. It is interesting to note also that American authors to which I have had access consider there is no liability apart from negligence. The opinions of these writers are, of course, not authoritative, but in default of others may be mentioned. In *The Law of the Honey Bee,* by Colin P.Campbell, LL.M., general counsel to the American Honey-Producers' League, 1924, the author says, at p. 33: "All the authorities make it clear that the true basis of liability for injuries done by bees is negligence on the part of the owner either in the location of the hives or in the manner of their manipulation." For this proposition he cites a number of cases in the American reports, the case of *O'Gorman v. O'Gorman* [1903] 2 Ir.R. 573, and a Canadian case, *Lucas v. Pettit* [1906] Ont. L.R. 448. In *Tellier v. Pelland* [1873] 5 R.L.N. 561 (Canada), which is referred to in the *English and Empire Digest* Vol. 2, p.252, the rule in *Rylands v. Fletcher* L.R. 3 H.L. 330 was applied to bees, but it appears from Mr Campbell's book, at p. 34, that this case is founded on statute law. *Lucas v. Pettit* [1906] Ont.L.R. 448 is also cited in the Digest and is to the same effect. The reports of the American and Canadian cases are not available, and I am therefore unable to obtain any assistance from them.

Accepting as I do, the authority of *O'Gorman v. O'Gorman* [1903] 2 Ir.R. 573, I am of the opinion that the true ground of action for damages in respect of injuries inflicted by bees is negligence, and that the Magistrate's decision was right. I think, however, that it is at least doubtful whether bees can be placed in the category of dangerous animals.

The appeal is therefore dismissed, with costs, £10. 10s.

Appeal dismissed.

Solicitors for the appellant: *Trip and Rolleston* (Timaru).
Solicitors for the respondents: *Raymond, Raymond, and Campbell* (Timaru). .

VI   England.
KEARRY v. PATTINSON

Editors' Introductory Notes.
The following cases dealt with similar circumstances:-
Harris v. Elder 1893. 57 J.P. 553
Quantrill v. Spragge 1907. 71 J.P.Jo 425.
Wenlock v. Curtis 1929. 73 S.J. 860
Hallett v. Jones 1935 80 L.J. 173
However the case of *Kearry v. Pattinson* deals with the matter so fully and

authoratively that the earlier cases are really no longer relevant.
For commentaries on the judgments in this case, see:-
E.J.Cohn in the Law Quarterly Review 1939 Vol CCXVIII p.289.
The Canadian Bar Review Vol 17 1939 pp.130-139 & 215 & 688
A Receiver of Stolen Property, Middle Temple, pp .21. Sir Kenneth Swan.
Slesser L.J. said that it is quite clear...that bees are *ferae naturae*
That there is really no authority for the proposition that the plaintiff had any right in
law to follow the bees on to another man's land without that other man's leave.
It follows therefore, that no action can be maintained by the plaintiff for conversion,
because he has no right in the bees.
Lord Goddard said that the question was as to what Blackstone meant when he says:
"and have power to pursue them."
He also said that if the animal gets on to another person's land, I have no right to
follow it on to that land, but if I do follow it I can retake the animal. I shall be once
more possessed of the animal, but I shall be liable in trespass to the owner of that
land because I have gone on to his land without any authority so to do.
It follows therefore, that you cannot demand entry upon another man's land for the
purpose of retaking animals.

REPORT
Of
KEARRY v. PATTINSON
[1939] 1 K. B. 471.
C.A. 1938. Dec. 20.

*Ferae naturae-Qualified ownership when hived-ownership of swarm-Right of
former owner to follow swarm on another man's land-Refusal by owner of land of
leave to enter upon land-Bees fly away-Action for conversion-Action for
infringement of legal right.*

Bees are ferae naturae, but when hived they become the qualified property of the
person who hives them. The owner of a swarm of bees has no legal right to follow the
bees on another man's land. When a swarm of bees settles on another person's land, the
former owner of the bees loses his right in them, which again become ferae naturae.

APPEAL from a decision of His Honour Judge Sir Reginald Banks sitting at the
Hull County Court.

The judgment of the county court judge, in which the facts are stated, was as
follows: The plaintiff Thomas Kearry, is a beekeeper. On June 16, 1938, about noon,
some of his bees swarmed, and settled in the garden of the defendant, Walter
Pattinson, who is his next door neighbour. I find that the plaintiff had not lost sight
of them, and could identify them, and they therefore remained his property. About 1
p.m. the plaintiff, accompanied by his brother and a Mr.Taylor, another beekeeper,
went to the defendant's house and asked the defendant's permission to go into his
garden and recover the bees. The defendant said: "No, you only speak to me when
you want something." It is a fact that the parties have been unfriendly for some
years, the plaintiff at one time having assaulted the defendant's wife. The plaintiff
went away. At 10 a.m. next morning the plaintiff, who is a postmen, saw the
defendant in the Post Office, and the defendant said: "The bees are on the hedge in
my garden close to the ground. You can get them by going across Mr. Fenton's
field." The plaintiff went to get his brother's help, but they decided not to cross Mr.
Fenton's field. The plaintiff says he was afraid of trespassing, but admits that he took

no steps to get permission from Fenton, who lives quite near to him.. He further says that he did not think he would be able to get at the bees from Fenton's field. About half an hour afterwards the plaintiff returned to the defendant and said: "I cannot trespass on Fenton's land and unless you allow me to come into your garden I shall not bother." The defendant then gave him permission and the plaintiff followed him into the garden. The bees had gone. There is no evidence that the defendant interfered with the bees or frightened them or shook them. All he did was to refuse to allow the plaintiff to enter his garden until the morning of June 17, when it was too late. The plaintiff sues for the loss of the swarm and loss of profit on the honey he would have got. I find 4*l.* is the proper sum if he has any right to claim anything. If the defendant had interfered with the bees and so disturbed them so as to destroy the plaintiff's chance of recovering them, then, in my opinion he would have been liable; but I do not think he committed any actionable wrong by a mere refusal to allow the plaintiff to go upon his land for the purpose of recovering his swarm. Judgment for the defendant with costs on Scale B.

The particulars of the plaintiff's claim were as follows: The plaintiff has suffered damage by the defendant on or about the 16th day of June, 1938, preventing the plaintiff from going on to the defendant's land and/or refusing permission for the plaintiff to go thereon for the purpose of recovering the property of the plaintiff - namely, a swarm of bees. The plaintiff claims damages for loss of the same 4*l.* The plaintiff also claims such further or other relief as the Court may deem fit.

The plaintiff appealed. The appeal was heard on December 20, 1938.

Ralph S. Shove for the appellant. The plaintiff has a right of action against the defendant for refusing to allow him to go upon his land in order to retake possession of his bees. The gist of the action is the failure of the defendant to deliver up to the plaintiff the property of the plaintiff or in preventing the plaintiff from exercising his right of ownership. The old authorities show that an action will lie for preventing a person taking possession of his property. Once bees have been hived they are the property of the person who hives them so long as he keeps them in sight. Blackstone in his Commentaries on the Laws of England, ed. 1766, Book II., ch. 25, p. 392, says: "Bees also are ferae naturae; but, when hived and reclaimed, a man may well have a qualified property in them, by the law of nature, as well as by the civil law. And to the same purpose, not to say in the same words, with the civil law, speaks Bracton: Occupation, that is, hiving or including them, gives the property in bees; for, though, a swarm lights upon my tree, I have no more property in them till I have hived them, than I have in the birds which make their nests thereon; and therefore if another hives them, he shall be their proprietor: but a swarm, which fly from and out of my hive, are mine so long as I can keep them in sight, and have power to pursue them; and in these circumstances no one else is entitled to take them."

[SLESSER L.J. What do the words "and have power to pursue them" mean?]

They mean that the bees have not flown beyond the reach of their owner. They do not mean that the owner has the legal right to go on to the land to take them. The quotation from Bracton in Blackstone is almost identical with what is stated in Justinian's Institutes Book, II., Title I., sect. 14, which according to Dr. Moyle's translation is as follows: "Bees again are naturally wild; hence if a swarm settles on your tree, it is no more considered yours, until you have hived it, than the birds which build their nests there, and consequently if it is hived by someone else, it becomes his property. . . . . A swarm which has flown from your hive is considered to remain yours so long as it is in your sight and easy of pursuit: otherwise it belongs to the first person who catches it." Inasmuch as the bees were the property of the plaintiff while on the defendant's land, the same law is applicable to them as to any other chattel. The defendant, having refused to deliver up to the plaintiff his bees, is liable to him in conversion as well as in detinue. The refusal to allow a person to retake possession of his own property is an actionable wrong. The manner in which the goods came into the defendant's possession is immaterial: see Salmond on Torts, 9th ed., p. 305. The bees came into the defendant's possession because they swarmed and flew on to his land and he refused to allow the plaintiff to come on to his land and retake them.

[GODDARD L.J. Why are bees any different from any other form of animals ferae naturae? Pheasants which have been reared on a man's land are the property of the man who rears them, but if they go on to another man's land they are lost to the owner.]

[SLESSER L.J. It was held by Bayley J. in *Hannam v. Mockett* (1824) 2 B. & C. 934, 944 that bees are property, and are the subject of larceny.]

Sir William Holdsworth in his History of English Law, 3rd ed., vol.iii., p. 326, cites cases from the Year Books: "In 1343 detinue for a horse was brought against executors personally. Grene afterwards said, 'In whatever way it (the horse) came into your possession, whether as executors, or because you took it out of the possession of some one else, or because you found it, if you detain it I shall have an action; whereupon, inasmuch as you do not answer as to the detinue, which is the principal matter of the action, judgment.' The other side were driven to traverse the fact that the horse had come into their possession and the detention. Y.B.17, 18 Edw.III. (R.S.) 514, 516. In 1344 there was another case in which the ground of action was not a bailment but a devenerunt ad manus. Y.B. 18 Edw.III. (R.S.) 214 seq. In 1371 detinue was brought for an ass. Y.B. 44 Edw. III. Pasch. pl. 30. The plaintiff counted that the ass strayed into the seignory of the defendant, who took the animal as an estray, that he had tendered a reasonable sum, and that the defendant had refused to deliver up the ass. Issue was taken on the sufficiency of the tender. No one seemed to suppose that detinue did not lie in such a case; and this is just such a case as would in older time have supported an action for res adiratae- the man had lost his property and it had come to the defendant's hands. In 1410 Thirning and Hill agreed that detinue lay against a stranger who found another's property and declined to restore it. Y.B. 11 Henry IV. Hil. pl. 20 (p. 46)". The case of the ass is exactly the same as the bees in the present case: it had come on to the defendant's land by straying; nevertheless it was held that, if the defendant did not deliver it up, the owner had an action for detinue against him. There is no authority which says that the owner of bees has the right to follow the bees when they swarm on to land invito the owner of the land.

[CLAUSON L.J. referred to *Gedge v. Minne* (1613) 2 Bulstrode, 60, 61., where it was said that "one may well pursue such a beast or vermin, when once he is up, and that into another mans ground, but a man cannot justifie his entering into another mans ground, to find, and so to hunt such a vermin, without his consent first had for the same, but he will be a trespasser for so doing 38 Ed. 3, fol. 10b. a man may follow his hawk or his hound in pursuit of the game, into another mans land, being found in his own, and by 12 Hen. 8, fol. 10, if a man flies his faulcon in his own land at a fesant, and he kills the fesant in anothers ground he may follow his hawk and take the fesant, and he is not to be punished but only for his entry into the others ground."]

It is stated in Viner's Abridgment under title "Trespass L a 6" that "if trees grow in my hedge, hanging over another man's land, and the fruit of them falls into the other's land, I may justify my entry to gather up the fruit, if I make no longer stay there than is convenient, nor break his hedge."

[CLAUSON L.J. referred to *Anthony v. Haney* (1832) 8 Bing. 186, which was an action for trespass for entering the plaintiff's close and pulling down and removing a barn. Plea that the defendant was the owner of the barn and that he entered to take his goods doing no unnecessary damage. It was held that the plea was bad in law.]

It has been held that to say of a man that he stole my bees was actionable as being a slander. Bees that are still in sight and are not difficult to pursue remain the property of their owner.

[SLESSER L.J. Sir H.S. Theobald K.C. in his work on The Law of Land, 2nd ed., says at p. 200: "Bracton was of opinion that if a man's bees kept in a hive, swarm, the swarm is his so long as he can follow it. But there is no reason to suppose that he can follow it on to another man's land without that other's leave. The swarm having left the hive becomes ferae naturae, and not the subject of property until hived."]

In America it has been decided that the owner of bees that swarm and fly on to the land of a third person retains his right to the bees: see *Goff v. Kilts* (1836) 15 Wendell (New York) 550, and *Brown v. Eckes* (1916) 160 N.Y. (Supp.) 489. So long as the swarm of bees is within the owner's sight and he has the physical power to pursue the bees he is still regarded as the owner of the bees, and can retake them. Bees are entirely different from any other animal, in so far as they split off from the rest of the bees and swarm.

[GODDARD L.J. When bees swarm they lose the instinct of revertendi. It was held by the Sheriff-Substitute in *Harris v. Elder* (1893) 57 J.P.(Journ.) 553 that, when bees swarmed from a hive, they remained the property of the owner so long as he was pursuing them where he was entitled to go, but that if the bees came upon another person's land, that person was entitled to prevent pursuit on his land, and that if the bees were hived by that person they became his property.]

The swarm of bees came into the hands of the owner of the land on which they swarmed. If the swarm had been hived by the defendant, it would have been the subject of larceny.

[SLESSER L.J. The whole Court are of opinion that in the circumstances of this case these bees were not the chattels of the plaintiff while they were on the defendant's hedge.]

In *Quantrill v. Spragge* (1907) 71 J.P. (Journ.) 425 the plaintiff claimed damages for the loss of a swarm of bees and the defendant claimed damages for the plaintiff's trespass on his garden. The county court judge held there was no damage to either party and ordered each to bear his own costs. It was held in *Van Toll v. Wall* (1859) 1 F. & F. 504 and in *Walker v. Clyde* (1861) 10 C.B. (N.S.) 381 that where a defendant prevented a person possessed of goods from removing them he was liable for conversion. The owner of bees which have swarmed and flown on to the land of a third person has the right to go on to the land of the third person in order to retake possession of the bees.

Alastair Sharp for the respondent was not called upon.

SLESSER L.J. This case is an interesting and an important one. It has been fully argued by Mr. Shove. In my view, as I have come to a certain conclusion which I shall mention in a few moments, many of the arguments which have been put before the Court on conversion and case do not arise for consideration.

The facts are these: The plaintiff, Thomas Kearry, is a beekeeper. On June 16, about noon, some of his bees swarmed and settled in the garden of the defendant, who was his next door neighbour. The learned county court judge tells us that the plaintiff went with his brother and another beekeeper to the defendant's house and asked the defendant's permission to go into his garden and recover these bees. The defendant refused. Later on, the next morning, the plaintiff having again seen the defendant, the defendant said: "The bees are on the hedge in my garden . You can get them by going across another man's field." The plaintiff decided not to attempt to go across the other man's field, fearing he would be a trespasser. Later on, upon returning to the defendant, the defendant eventually gave the plaintiff permission to follow the defendant into the garden, but by that time the bees had flown away. Upon that an action was brought and damages were claimed. The case was framed in this way, that the plaintiff had suffered damage by the defendant, on or about June 16, preventing the plaintiff from going on to the defendant's land and refusing permission to the plaintiff to go thereon for the purpose of recovering the property of the plaintiff, namely a swarm of bees, and damages 4l. and an ordinary claim for further and other relief. When the case was argued before the learned county court judge it was not put, as I read the judgment, so much upon the basis of a claim for invasion of a legal right as upon the basis of conversion. However it may be put, the basic question is whether these bees at the material time were chattels at all.

It is quite clear, as is pointed out by Blackstone in his Commentaries upon the Laws of England, ed. (1766), Book II, ch. 25, p.392 that bees are ferae naturae. That is the view taken both in the civil law to be found in the Institutes of Justinian, Book ii., Title I., Sect. 14, and in Bracton, who, as we all know, so largely founded himself upon the civil law, but as the result of hiving there is a well known exception to that general rule. It is stated in this way by Blackstone, and is in agreement, as I read it, with the earlier authorities. "Bees" he writes "are ferae naturae; but when hived and reclaimed, a man may have a qualified property in them, by the law of nature, as well as by the civil law. And to the same purpose, not to say in the same words, with the civil law, speaks Bracton: Occupation, that is, hiving or including them, gives the property in bees; for though a swarm lights upon my tree, I have no more property in them till I have hived them, than I have in the birds which make their nests thereon; and therefore if another hives them, he shall be their proprietor: but a swarm, which flies from and out of my hive, are mine so long as I can keep them in sight, and have power to pursue them; and in these circumstances no one else is entitled to take them." There is no doubt in this case that these bees had been hived by the plaintiff. Before they swarmed they were his property (see *Hannam v. Mockett* 2 B. & C. 934,944), and the bees when they swarmed, so long as they were in his sight and so long as he had power to pursue them, would remain his property. But what do these words "have power to pursue them" mean? It appears, when the authorities are searched, that there is really no authority for the proposition that the plaintiff had any right in law to follow the bees on to another man's land without that other man's leave. The cases which have been cited to us where a man has been held in the past to have had some special right to follow particular animals, do not meet this point. We have looked at the case of *Gedge v. Minne* 2 Bulstrode, 60, which is said to be an authority for the proposition that a man may enter upon another man's land to recover his hound or hawk when they have escaped into that land. I do not wish to discuss that case; it seems to be based in part upon certain rights in the owner of hawks and hounds to follow them in pursuit of game (see Y.B. 38 Edw. 3, fol. 10b.,

40

and Y.B. 12 Hen. 8, fol. 10), and in part upon a consideration of common interest and the like; I see no reason to extend it so as to give a right to the owner of bees to pursue a swarm on to another man's land. The only ownership of bees is rationale soli, to which may be added a power lawfully where possible without difficulty to recapture. Thus a qualified property may be had in bees in consideration of the property whereon they are found: 2 Bl. Com. 392; Bro. Abr. Tit. Propertie: *Tibbs v. Smith* (1661) T. Raym. 33, but there is no right to pursue a swarm of bees on to another man's land and such pursuit would amount to a trespass. I cannot help thinking that the power to pursue them which constitutes them chattels referred to in the old books means and can only mean that they may still be so regarded when the swarm is in such a place that their owner has still in law the right to pursue them in order to recapture them. They are ferae naturae before being hived, but they may be taken into the disposition of the owner per industriam by hiving and so become his property: see Pufendorf De Jure Naturae et Gentium, Book IV., ch. 6, s.5, but may remain his property while they are swarming so long as they are in his sight and he has lawful power easily to pursue them. So I read the authorities. For that reason I think this action is misconceived, because the bees at the time of the action of the defendant complained of had ceased to be in the disposition or power of the plaintiff altogether. It follows, therefore, that no action can be maintained by the plaintiff for conversion, because he has no property in the bees, and secondly, inasmuch as he had not the right to follow the bees on to the defendant's land, the defendant had not invaded any right the plaintiff had in refusing to allow him access and therefore no action in case could have been founded. Whether the action be founded in conversion or for the infringement of a right, it fails and the appeal should be dismissed.

CLAUSON L.J. I agree.

GODDARD L.J. I agree. We have had an interesting discussion in this case, and it is evidently regarded as one of some importance, but the point sought to be made which was argued before the learned county court judge really is based on an entirely false premise. It is based on a mis-reading of a passage in Blackstone. The passage in Blackstone's Commentaries which is relied upon in this case is in Book II., ch. 25, p. 392, in the 4th ed., where Blackstone speaks of the property in animals which are ferae naturae. He then refers to bees and says that there may be a qualified property in bees, that is a property once they have been reduced into possession so long as they are in the hive. Then he deals with what happens when bees swarm, that is when they leave the hive, and go off and no longer return to the hive, as they do once they have swarmed and have been hived. He says: "Though a swarm lights upon my tree, I have no more property in them till I have hived them, than I have in the birds which make their nests thereon; and therefore if another hives them, he shall be their proprietor." If bees settle on my tree and another person manages to get on to my land and hives them, they become that person's property. How much more would one expect them to be that person's property if the bees fly on to that person's land and he hives them there. It is said: But a swarm which fly out from my hive are mine so long as I have power to pursue them. The whole of this argument comes down to what Blackstone means when he says : "and have power to pursue them." In my view he is there saying no more than that the law with regard to bees is the same as it is with regard to any other wild creature which is reduced into possession and in which a man has a qualified property so long as he keeps it in possession. If a wild deer which lives in my park gets out, I am at liberty to pursue it and get it back. I dare say that while I am pursuing it another person has not a right to come between me and the animal, so as to prevent me retaking it. If, however, that animal gets on to another person's land, I have no right to follow it on to that land, but if I do follow it I can retake the animal; I shall be once more possessed of the animal, but I shall be liable in trespass to the owner of that land because I have gone on to his land without any authority so to do. It follows, therefore, that you cannot demand entry upon another man's land for the purpose of retaking animals. The third edition of Bullen and Leake on Pleading shows there is no case to be found in the books for any plea justifying a trespass on the ground that the trespasser was pursuing an animal, or indeed any other property, for the purpose of retaking it. There is a plea justifying a trespass on the ground that the trespasser was exercising a right under a grant to hunt an animal, but there is no case to be found in any book suggesting that any one has a right to go upon the land of another man to retake an animal ferae naturae. In my judgment the defendant was under no obligation whatever to allow the plaintiff to come on his land to get the bees. On the other hand the defendant was entitled, if he chose, after the bees had come on to his land, to reduce them into possession, and keep them for himself. In my judgment the bees had never been in the defendant's possession and never could be regarded as in his possession until he had put them into a skip or a hive himself.

For these reasons I think the learned county court judge was right in the conclusion to which he came, although I do not agree with the view that he expressed. I say this in case the view he expressed should mislead other people. I do not agree that, if the defendant interfered with the bees when they got on to his land, that would give any cause of action to the plaintiff.

Appeal dismissed.

Solicitors for appellant: *Hamlins, Grammer & Hamlin.*
Solicitors for respondent: *Smith & Hudson, for Richard Whitty & Co., Hull.*

R.F.S.

VII   **1946. U.S.A.**
                    HOLDEN v. LEWIS

Editors' Introductory Notes.

Sweney, J. said that the keeping of bees is not in itself a nuisance. He held that the action before him was one to restrain a nuisance; there was no allegation of negligence; for the plaintiffs to succeed it was incumbent on them to show that they were subjected to unreasonable inconvenience, hurt and annoyance as a result of the defendants' keeping of their bees. The court did not feel that the plaintiffs had proved anything beyond the fact that certain people in the neighbourhood had been stung by bees, hornets, wasps and yellow jackets. There were other colonies of bees and hornets, wasps and bumble bees in the neighbourhood, the damage might have caused by these rather than by the beekeeper's bees.

This is an interesting case which shows that the neighbour must not only prove that he is enduring what can amount to a legal nuisance but he must also satisy the court that it is the defendant's bees which cause the problem. More may be needed than the unsupported statements of the people stung. It was stated that negligence was irrelevant in a nuisance case but this point can be disputed.

REPORT
Of
HOLDEN v. LEWIS
(1946) 56 Pa D. & C. 639.
[Also reported 33 Del Co 458]
District and County Reports.
[639 (1946)]

Holden et Ux. v. Lewis et ux.

Nuisances - Keeping of bees in residential neighborhood - Evidence - Burden of proof.

1. The keeping of bees is not a nuisance per se, although the keeping of an unreasonable number of bees in an unreasonable place may be a nuisance.

2. In a bill in equity for injunction to restrain defendants from continuing the keeping of bees on the premises occupied by them in a residential neighborhood averring that the bees stung and harassed plaintiffs and their minor children and that the keeping of the bees constituted a nuisance, plaintiffs had the burden of proving that they were subjected to unreasonable inconvenience and annoyance as a result of defendants keeping the bees, and the bill will be dismissed where plaintiffs' evidence amounted to no more than a showing that their children as well as other people in the neighborhood had been stung by bees, hornets, wasps and yellow jackets, there being evidence also that other beehives were kept by persons in the neighborhood and no evidence that the bees which harassed the plaintiffs belonged to defendants.

Bill in Equity. C. P. of Delaware County, June term, 1945, No. 78

William Taylor, Jr., for plaintiffs.

Bruce W. Long, for defendants.

SWENEY, J., January 7, 1946.-

Statement of pleadings

Plaintiffs, Thomas A. Holden and Anna Louise Holden, his wife, filed a bill in equity for an injunction restraining defendants, George R. Lewis and Elizabeth Lewis, his wife, from continuing the keeping of bees on premises occupied by them, and situate in Newtown Township, this county.

The bill alleges that the parties to the action reside on Mulberry Lane, Valley View Acres, Newtown Township, this county; that that section of the township has been developed as a residential district, and is built up with dwellings; that defendants, or one of them, keep and maintain hives of bees on their premises in such numbers and in such proximity to the home of plaintiffs, and the homes of other residents in the community, that the bees fly to and from the premises of plaintiffs; that the bees sting, menace and harass plaintiffs and their minor children, and sting and menace the owners and occupiers of adjacent properties; that the keeping of bees and the consequent annoyance, inconvenience and harm caused to plaintiffs and their children constitutes a nuisance; that in consequence of the foregoing, plaintiffs are deprived of the free and reasonable use and enjoyment of their home and property; that plaintiffs are without an adequate remedy at law.*

*The Rules of Equity Practice provide as follows: "The Combination clause, the interrogatories, the allegation of a want of remedy at law, and all other formal averments, must be omitted": Rule 34. In Weir v. Potter Title and Mortgage Guarantee Co., 323 Pa. 212, the Court said at p. 217: "These rules are mandatory."

Defendants filed an answer in which they admit that one of them, namely, George

R. Lewis, keeps and maintains one hive of bees on defendants' premises, the number of bees in said hive varying from time to time so that it is impossible to give the exact number in said hive. The answer denies that the bees kept and maintained by George R. Lewis sting, menace and harass plaintiffs and their minor children, or that they sting and menace the owners and occupiers of adjacent properties; denies that the keeping of the bees, and the alleged consequent annoyance, inconvenience and harm caused to plaintiffs and their children, constitute a nuisance; and denies that plaintiffs are deprived of the free and reasonable use of their home and property by reason of the bees kept and maintained by George R. Lewis.

On September 21, 1945, a hearing was held before the writer of this adjudication, and the testimony has been transcribed and filed of record.

The single issue raised by the pleadings is: Does the maintenance of the bees by defendants, or by defendant, George R. Lewis, alone, on defendants' premises, constitute a nuisance?

From the admissions in the pleadings and the evidence taken at the hearing, we make the following

Findings of fact

1. Plaintiffs are husband and wife, and reside at 4 Mulberry Lane, Valley View Acres, Newtown Township, Delaware County, Pennsylvania.
2. Defendants are husband and wife, and reside at 12 Mulberry Lane, Valley View Acres, Newtown Township, Delaware County, Pennsylvania.
3. The section of the township where the parties to this action reside has been developed as a residential district. Mulberry Lane, Valley View Acres, is a strictly suburban residential development, composed of single houses located on lots having a frontage of 65 feet on Mulberry Lane, and a depth of 112 feet, with but one house to a lot.
4. The husband defendant keeps and maintains a hive of bees in the back yard of the premises where defendants reside. The distance from his hive to the nearest point on the plaintiff's premises is about 255 feet.
5. Bee hives are kept and maintained by other persons in the neighborhood. One hive is located at a distance of about 600 feet from plaintiff's residence. Another resident in the community maintains nine hives of bees approximately two squares from plaintiff's residence.
6. In addition to the bees kept by residents in the community, there are the usual number of hornets, wasps and bumble bees ordinarily found in the suburbs.
7. On occasion, bees hornets, wasps and other insects fly over and above the yards and lawns of the residents, and sting, harass and annoy persons, especially small children. Very small children are sometimes frightened, and their parents are reluctant to leave them outdoors. On rare occasions, older persons are forced to leave their lawns and yards and go indoors.

Discussion

The keeping of bees is not a nuisance per se. The keeping of an unreasonable number of bees in an unreasonable place may be a nuisance: Town of Arkadelphia v. Clark, 52 Ark. 23; Allman v. Rexer, 21 D. & C. 431. However, their mere existence does not make them such.

"The difference between a business, which, no matter how it is conducted, is a nuisance per se as to certain location and surrounding, and a business which is being so conducted as to become a nuisance, lies in the proof, not in the remedy. In the former, the right to relief is established by averment and proof of the mere act; in the other, proof of the act and its consequences is necessary:..." Pennsylvania Co. v. Sun Co., 290 Pa 404, 410.

It was incumbent on the plaintiffs, therefore, to prove that they were subjected to *unreasonable* inconvenience, hurt and annoyance as a result of *defendants'* keeping of their bees. After several readings of the testimony, we are unable to find that plaintiffs have met this burden of proof. The evidence undoubtedly supports the finding that bees, hornets, wasps, yellow jackets and other insects do invade the properties of the plaintiffs and others in the neighborhood; do sometimes sting and otherwise annoy persons therein, particularly small children; and do occasion some degree of fright in the children and some degree of anxiety on the part of parents for their children. All this may be conceded. But we are unable to find from the evidence that the husband defendant's bees are solely, or even partly, responsible for the discomfort, annoyance and inconvenience of which plaintiffs and their witnesses complain. Certainly, the husband defendant cannot be charged with liability for the action of hornets and wasps. The husband plaintiff testified to six occasions, during the past two years, when his children were stung. He freely admitted that he had seen yellow jackets, hornets and wasps around his property; and, when asked if he knew what stung his children, testified, "In some cases, we know they were wasps." Nor is the husband defendant responsible for the conduct of bees kept by other residents in the community. Under cross-examination, the husband plaintiff testified as follows:

"Q. You can't say of your own knowledge whether on any of these six occasions, your children were stung by a bee from Mr. Lewis' hive?

"A. No. That's impossible. Mr. Lewis, himself, would say bees don't carry signs."

Notwithstanding this testimony, plaintiffs' counsel asks us to find as a fact that Mr. Lewis's bees stung plaintiff's children. It may be admitted that the identity of a particular bee is difficult to establish. Nevertheless, difficulty of proof does not dispense with the necessity for it. The husband plaintiff's testimony is confused and contradictory. At one place, he testified that he was never "personally" disturbed by the bees. In the next breath, he stated: "The bees have stung me, and I wasn't bothering the bees."

Much of the evidence adduced by plaintiffs is of no value whatever. For the most part, it consists of the witnesses' bare conclusion that the bees that did the stinging belonged to defendants. For example, the entire direct examination of Mrs. Shearn, on the merits of the case, is as follows:

"Q. Have your sons or have they not ever had any encounters with these bees?

"A. Yes. They have been stung several times this year and last year."

There is no way of knowing that this witness understood by "these bees", whether the bees of defendants, the bees of other persons in the vicinity, or the bees belonging to no particular owner but which are usually found in any suburban area. If the witness meant the bees of this husband defendant, then her testimony that it was his bees which stung her sons was nothing more than a conclusion. No attempt whatsoever was made to trace the flight of the particular bee or bees involved. If it is claimed that the case was difficult of proof, then the case was one which required corresponding care in its preparation and presentation.

The testimony of Mrs. Shearn was typical of most of plaintiffs' evidence. Plaintiffs seem to rely upon several circumstances established by the evidence. In the first place, they point out that they were not bothered by stingings to any extent until defendants acquired their bees. They argue, therefore, that it must be defendants' bees that are responsible for their distress and discomfort. This argument loses whatever force it might otherwise have had in view of the husband plaintiff's admission that his children, on several of the six occasions when they were stung, were stung by wasps. Furthermore, when we consider that there were at least 10 other hives within two squares of plaintiff's home, it imposes an intolerable strain on human credulity to believe that only those bees kept by the husband defendant are the culprits.

Next, plaintiffs rely upon what may be called the physical characteristics of the neighborhood. The rear of the properties in Mulberry Lane backs up to the rear of the properties on Valley View Road, the next street over. The area composed of the back yards of the properties on these two streets forms what some of the witnesses called an "amphitheatre". It is argued that Mr. Lewis's bees fly up and down this area-way between the barriers formed by the houses on the two streets; and that neither his bees can get out of, nor other bees enter, this space. It so happens that the ten hives of bees owned by others than Mr.. Lewis are outside of the "amphitheatre". We believe that this circumstance is altogether insufficient to support any inference favorable to plaintiffs. The houses on Mulberry Lane and on Valley View Road do not occupy the entire width of the lot; there is considerable space between each house. There is, so far as the evidence discloses, nothing to prevent bees from flying over the houses, if they so will. We do not believe that bees in their flight are circumscribed by any such limitations as plaintiffs suggest. Freedom of movement seems to us to be one of their most pronounced characteristics, along with their indefatigable industry.

Plaintiffs produced testimony to show that in June 1945 a swarm of bees alighted on their premises. Whether or not these bees stung plaintiff's children, or one of them, is not altogether clear. At any rate, the swarm was removed, with Mrs. Holden's permission, by Mr. Lewis. The wife plaintiff testified that Mr. Lewis admitted at that time that the bees were from his hive. Mr. Lewis denied making any such admission. Even conceding that the testimony will support a finding that defendants' bees did swarm on plaintiff's premises on this occasion, plaintiffs have not established their right to an injunction. Equity will act only where the evidence shows repeated, constantly recurring trespasses; Stewart and Foltz's Appeal, 56 Pa. 413.

While it may be that the evidence discloses that plaintiffs, and others in the neighborhood, are subjected to a greater degree of annoyance and inconvenience from bees than is usual in communities of this rural character, we cannot find that plaintiffs have shown that defendants, or either of them, are responsible for this condition. Plaintiffs have failed to meet the burden of proof resting upon them.

"The burden of proof resting upon plaintiffs in civil actions cannot be met by conjectures. The phrase 'burden of proof' means exactly what it says. There is a close relationship in logic between the quality of proof required in criminal cases and that required in civil cases. The difference is in the degree of its cogency. In *both* classes of cases *proof* is required of the party on whom is the burden of establishing the truth of the basic proposition essential to recovery. Mere conjecture or guesses do not supply this proof. Circumstantial evidence is legal evidence in both classes of cases, but just as in a *criminal* case 'the evidence of facts and circumstances must be such as to excluded to a moral certainty, every hypothesis but that of guilt of the offense imputed' (Com. v. Benz, 318 Pa. 465,472, 178 A. 390), so in a *civil* case the evidence of facts and circumstances on which plaintiff relies and the inferences logically deducible therefrom, must so preponderate in favor of the basic proposition he is seeking to establish as to exclude any equally well supported belief in any inconsistent proposition." : DeReeder et al. v. Travelers Insurance Co., 329 Pa. 328,333.

Defendants' counsel expended considerable effort to show that his clients were not negligent in maintaining their bees. This should not have been done. The question of negligence was completely irrelevant. The bill charged defendants with maintaining a nuisance. It did not charge negligence. As to the distinction between nuisance, negligence and trespass, see Kramer v. Pittsburgh Coal Co., 341 Pa. 379.

Conclusions of law

1. The court has jurisdiction of the parties and the subject matter of this suit.
2. The bill should be dismissed with costs on plaintiffs.

Decree nisi

And now, January 7, 1946, upon consideration of the foregoing case, it is ordered, adjudged and decreed as follows:

1. That the bill of complaint be, and the same is, hereby dismissed.
2. That plaintiffs shall pay the costs of these proceedings.

Opinion sur exceptions

SWENEY, J. April 4, 1946. - Plaintiffs filed exceptions to the adjudication of the chancellor and the exceptions have been argued before the court en banc and are now ready for an opinion.

Plaintiffs filed a bill in equity to restrain defendants from keeping bees on their property in Newtown Township, this county; the bill alleged that the parties lived in a newly developed residential district; that defendants were keeping bees; that the bees had stung, menaced and harassed the plaintiffs, their children and their neighbors; that the keeping of bees constituted a nuisance and deprived plaintiffs of the rightful use of their property.

Upon answer filed, testimony was heard and the chancellor, on January 7, 1946 filed his findings of fact, and conclusions of law and decree nisi.

Plaintiffs excepted to the decree nisi, and the failure of the chancellor to find the plaintiffs' fifth, sixth, seventh and eighth requests for finding of fact and plaintiffs' first request for a conclusion of law.

Plaintiffs' fifth request for finding of fact was:

"The bees fly over and above the yards of the adjacent property owners, whose houses, on Valley View Road and Mulberry Lane, are so arranged that they form a kind of amphitheatre above the land comprising their respective rear lawns."

Plaintiffs' sixth request for finding of fact was:

"Within this area defendants' bees sting, annoy and frighten the neighbors, especially the small children, who on numerous occasions, since the hive has been located in defendants' yard, have been stung. Owing to this condition, plaintiffs have been obliged to give up their pracrice of having their four-year-old daughter rest on a cot in the yard, pursuant to medical advice."

Plaintiffs' seventh request for finding of fact was:

"With virtually no inconvenience to himself or detriment to the bees, defendant could remove the hive to some other location sufficiently remote to end the annoyance and inconvenience now occasioned to the neighbors by having the bees on defendants' land and within the semi-enclosure before referred to."

Plaintiffs' eight request for finding of fact was:

"The hive might either be taken back to the Ardlinger orchard, where it previously was kept, or it might be taken to the orchard of Dunwoody Home where the bees would serve a useful purpose in the pollination of the trees. Both places are readily accessible to the defendant and sufficiently removed to end the vexation complained of."

Plaintiffs' request for conclusion of law was:

"Under the circumstances of this case, it is unreasonable for defendant to keep his hive of bees in the location where he does, namely, his back yard, when, with slight inconvenience to himself, defendant by removing the hive to another location, could continue to keep bees without annoying the neighbors."

From these requests, it is apparent that plaintiffs feel that their testimony has shown (1) that the defendant husband's bees are confined in an amphitheatre; (2) that plaintiffs, their children and their neighbors have been stung and frightened thereby; (3) that the bees can be removed to one of two neighboring orchards, without much inconvenience to the defendant husband; and that the necessary legal conclusion to be drawn is that the defendant husband is unreasonable in not moving the bees.

As the chancellor pointed out in his adjudication, this is an action to restrain a nuisance; there is no allegation of negligence; and, it is incumbent upon plaintiffs to show that they were subjected to unreasonable inconvenience, hurt and annoyance as a result of *defendants'* keeping of their bees. We do not feel that plaintiffs have proved anything beyond the fact that certain people in their neighborhood have been stung by bees, hornets, wasps and yellow jackets and, this being the fact, we cannot find the facts or reach the conclusion of law which plaintiffs request.

Plaintiffs' exception one is dismissed, because we are convinced that the decree nisi should be made final. Plaintiffs' exceptions two, three, four and five are dismissed because they are requests for findings of fact which are unsupported by the testimony. Plaintiffs' exception six is dismissed, because it requests a conclusion of law to be drawn, which is not based on the facts of this case and is not supported by the law.

Final Decree

And now, April 4, 1946, it is ordered, adjudged and decreed as follows:
1. That the bill of complaint be, and the same is hereby dismissed.
2.   That plaintiffs shall pay the costs of these proceedings.

VIII   1950. England.
JOHNSON v. MARTIN

Editors' Introductory Notes

The judge, His Honour Judge Lawson Campbell said that in order to establish liability for nuisance it was necessary for the Plaintiff to show that the Defendant kept his bees in an unreasonable place, or had kept an unreasonable number of them The mere fact that he kept insects which could in certain circumstances, cause damage was not enough, for beekeeping was an ordinary use of land.

The Editorial Note at the end of the report is by the editor of the New Law Journal. *Damnum sine injuria* means damage without a legal remedy.

REPORT
Of
JOHNSON v. MARTIN
THE LAW JOURNAL SEPT 29TH 1950 p.541
COUNTY COURTS' REPORTER
Edited by O.M.W.Swingland, Esq., Barrister-at-Law.

27. Nuisance: Bee-keeping.

In *Johnson v. Martin,* at Cambridge County Court, HIS HONOUR JUDGE LAWSON CAMPBELL held that the plaintiff was unable to recover damages in respect of the death of a goat and injuries to other goats and to herself caused by the defendant's bees. On August 2, 1949, the plaintiff found that her goats were being attacked by a large number of bees. She went to their rescue, and was herself badly stung as a consequence of which she had to go to a hospital and was ill for a week. One goat died, and the others were injured. The Court found as a fact that the bees concerned belonged to the defendant. The parties occupied houses near a main road, separated by another house. All the houses had long narrow strips of land at the back, and behind the defendant's strip of garden there was a copse in which he kept a large number of bees. At the back of the plaintiff's garden and adjacent to the copse, there was the plaintiff's field in which she tethered her goats. The defendant's hives, which numbered forty-five and housed some 750,000 bees, were surrounded by tall bushes except in one place on the side adjacent to the plaintiff's field, where there was a gap which had been filled with brushwood. There was no evidence that the defendant had managed his bees in other than a proper manner; he had carried out a routine inspection two or three days before the occurrence, and had not thereafter done anything to affect the bees' habits or way of life. The Court held that there was no substance in the allegation of negligence. JUDGE LAWSON CAMPBELL said that in order to establish liability for nuisance it was necessary for the plaintiff to show that the defendant kept his bees in an unreasonable place, or had kept an unreasonable number of them. The mere fact that he kept insects which could in certain circumstances cause damage was not enough, for beekeeping was an ordinary use of land. The district was entirely agricultural, and dwellinghouses were few and remote from the copse where the hives were. The evidence was that the site was ideal. The number of bees was very large, but it seemed that even half the number of bees kept could have done the damage complained of: and it would be difficult to maintain that it was unreasonable to have kept half the number. The experts were of the opinion that there were certain conditions under which bees would attack goats, and they had given reasons for thinking that on the day in question those conditions had existed. If that was so, then a comparatively small number of bees, a number which could not be said to be unreasonable, could have caused identical damage.

Johnson v. Martin

Cambridge County Court Plaint No F.2253
Judgment Delivered June 28 1950.
Counsel: D.C.BAIN (for the plaintiff); E.GARTH.MOORE (for the defendant)
Solicitors: Wooton & Wallis, Cambridge (for the plaintiff); Few & Kester, Cambridge (for the defendant).
EDITORIAL NOTE [by Editor of the Law Journal]
The answer to the plaintiff's claim was that the defendant was properly exercising his right to keep bees, and, therefore, the plaintiff had suffered *damnum sine injuria.* Bee-keeping is regarded in the circumstances as an ordinary use of the land, and it follows that, unless the place where the bees were kept was not reasonably proper or the number was unreasonable, the plaintiff had suffered no wrong.

IX   **1966 . England.**
INGAMELLS v. PICKFORD
Editors' Introductory Notes.

There are several errors in the original of this report but it is helpful in spite of this. The errors include the Judge's name and the date of the case of *Parker v. Reynolds*. These two have been corrected.

The judge discounted the stings received by the workmen as he considered that they had contributed to their misfortune.

Soiling of washing he considered to be minor and occasional. Nothing could be done about it.

Referring to stings he averaged the number of stings at two stings per year; this he did not consider exceptional in this country.

REPORT
Of
INGAMELLS v. PICKFORD
BEE CRAFT: SEPTEMBER & OCTOBER 1966

At Leicester County Court on Jan 24, an action was brought by Mr. B. Ingamells of 376 Gipsy Lane, Leicester against Mr. F.W.Pickford of 378 Gipsy Lane, seeking damages of £100 and an injunction to restrain him from keeping bees at 9 Edgehill Road. The case was heard by His Honour Judge Robson Q.C.

The case was opened by Mr Geoffrey Jones for the plaintiff, who said that some 110,000 bees were kept on the garage and in the garden adjoining his client's property and these were a nuisance. He sought to establish a precedent by reference to three cases; one in Canada in 1895, one in Ireland and a third at Birmingham County Court. The latter was in the form of a newspaper clipping of unknown date. [Is this a reference to *Parker v. Reynolds*? Eds.] He also drew a parallel of cockerels crowing in 1939 and a case in 1699 of pigs which stank so much that a neighbour could not use his land. In both cases injunctions had been granted. Mr. Jones argued that a similar case was presented by the flight of bees from two hives on the garage roof, and from two hives in the garden which prevented his client from enjoying the full use of his property.

Mr. A. Ball for the defence sought to prove that the bees were not a nuisance and quoted a case from the January issue of Bee Craft. He stated that no other complaint had been made about the bees in the ten years they had been in this position, particularly by the previous occupier of 376 Gipsy Lane.

The first witness was Mr. Ingamells, who stated that he had occupied this property for three and a half years, and he had approached the defendant and asked him to remove the bees in the summer of 1964, following an incident when workmen had been stung twelve times while laying a lawn. The work had taken six days instead of three. He also stated that he was unable to use the lawn, and that bees invaded his greengrocer's shop in search of flowers, and deterred customers from entering.

Under cross-examination he admitted that he could not tell whether an Italian bee shown to him was a wasp or a bee. He also admitted that the flowers were in the doorway, and that wasps entered the shop during the late summer.

Mrs. Ingamells then gave evidence that she was afraid to go into the garden, and referred to an occasion when Mrs Pickford asked her not to go into the garden as the bees were swarming. She also said that she could not have flowers in the garden because people said they would attract bees.

Mr. Ingamells senior was the next witness, and he quoted an occasion when he and his son were drinking beer on the lawn, and he was stung once while his son was stung four times.

Corroborative evidence was given by a witness from the contractors regarding the workmen.

The first witness for the defence was Mr. F.W.Pickford. He said that he had kept approximately the same number of hives in the same position for the last ten years. He had had no complaints until the present occupier moved into 376 Gipsy Lane, and then only after two years. Defence counsel asked what type of bees were kept. Witness said that they were Italians, and easily confused with wasps by the uninitiated. The Judge intervened to ask if the defendant was still suggesting that the stings were caused by wasps, since the plaintiff had referred to removing the sting on each occasion. Witness agreed that the stings were bee stings. Mr. Pickford then stated that on one occasion a dustbin was set as near to the hives as possible, and set on fire so that smoke enveloped the hives. On the day that the lawn was being laid, a youth sprayed water from a hose in front of the hives, frequently directing a jet into the hive entrances. Mr. Pickford was asked by Mr. Jones if he would agree that it was unpleasant to be stung by a neighbour's bees. In his reply he said that it was remarkable that the plaintiff was never stung until he decided to take legal action. Counsel then demanded if witness suggested the plaintiff was not telling the truth, or if he accepted the evidence. The witness replied that he must accept the evidence.

The case was then adjourned until the following day when the first witness was the headmaster of the school across Gipsy Lane from the premises. He stated that he had 450 children on roll, of whom about 300 crossed Gipsy Lane and passed in front of 378 and 376 Gipsy Lane. Of these approximately half turned down Edgehill Road and passed in front of the garage on which the hives were situated. He had had two wasp stings reported last year, but no bee stings since he had been headmaster. The Judge remarked that he supposed he heard almost all that had happened to the children. He replied "Too true, your Honour".

The next witness lived until recently at 380 Gipsy Lane. She stated that she had never had any trouble caused by bees during the seven years she occupied the premises.

A further witness gave evidence that he knew nothing about bees, but was a frequent visitor at 378 Gipsy Lane and often crossed the garden to 9 Edgehill Road. On one occasion he had helped to hive a swarm. He had never found the bees aggressive nor had he been stung.

Mr. Benson, chairman of Leicestershire and Rutland B.K.A. then took the stand as an expert witness. In his evidence he suggested that the erection of a wire netting fence twelve feet high by the defendant might be a mistake, since bees might hit it and become annoyed. He also said that bees went to Mr. Ingamell's drain for water. This could be prevented by a few drops of sanitary fluid.

He explained that soiling of washing at Mrs. Ingamells, which would be a rare occurrence, did not happen to Mrs. Pickford because bees do not defæcate until they were some distance from the hive. The Judge here interposed that this disposed of a conflict of evidence on this point by the two parties, which had been puzzling him.

Mr. Benson, questioned by Mr. Jones, said that a garage roof ten feet high was an ideal place to keep bees. He himself had two hives in a similar position. To further questions he said that he did not get complaints, except on one occasion when he dropped a hive.

Counsel then made their closing speeches. During that of Mr. Jones a further reference to stinking pigs, and crowing cockerels drew a comment by Judge Robson - "Yes, Mr. Jones, but you see bees don't do anything. They don't smell or make a noise." The Judge also said that he could not understand why there were no references available of previous cases. Those quoted were colonial, and useful in their way, as were the cuttings, but he had been unable to find any reference to previous English cases. He had spent some time searching on the previous evening. He then commented "You see I have nothing to go on." His Honour then said that he was wondering if the bees stung the workmen because they were spraying them with water or if the workmen sprayed the bees because they were being stung. As the witness from the contractors had left, he recalled Mr Benson to the stand and questioned him on this point, coming to the conclusion that the workmen contributed to their own discomfort.

The Judge closed the hearing at the end of the second day, saying that he had a lot to think about and that he would delay his judgment until he sat in that Court next time.

The case was resumed on March 7th, when a surprise application was made by Mr. Jones for the recall of Mr. Benson. After legal argument whether it was permissible, Judge Robson pointed out that he had had a month to decide his findings, and asked on what point Mr. Jones wished to question Mr. Benson. Mr. Jones said that as a result of the publicity a letter had been received contradicting his statement that he had had no trouble with his neighbours. In fact solicitors letter had passed between them. The Judge pointed out that the witness had said he did have trouble *when he dropped a hive.* Upon this Mr. Jones withdrew his application.

The summing up by His Honour Judge Robson was concise and dealt with each item of evidence. He based his findings on a case in 1905 [1906 Eds.] before a brother Judge at Birmingham, which his researches had found, and in which an injunction had been granted. He held this to be the law on bees in England at the present time. He said that when the case commenced he expected to hear of continuous swarms. Only one swarm had been mentioned and no complaint had been made about this. In fact, the defendant's wife told Mrs. Ingamells not to go into the garden as the bees were swarming. He felt that whilst the bees were probably harmless it was much wiser for people not used to them to avoid them and it seemed to him a sensible suggestion. He thought the defendant had acted in good faith in erecting a fence to cause the bees to fly higher and planting Russian Vines to grow over it; although it might have done more harm than good according to the expert. In his opinion the growth shown in one season (in photographs) meant that the wire netting would soon be replaced by a hedge. He discounted the stings received by the workmen as he considered they had contributed to their misfortunes. Soiling of washing he considered to be minor and occasional. Nothing could be done about this. Referring to stings he averaged the number at two stings per year, this he did not consider exceptional in this country.

He felt sorry for the plaintiff, but there was nothing in law he could do about it. The Judge then found for the defendant, and awarded costs against the plaintiff.

X   **1982. England.**
TUTTON & OTHERS v. A.D. WALTER LTD
Editors' Introductory Notes.

Unfortunately we do not have room in this volume to give a full copy of the report of this case. However, we give a copy of the headnote which sets out the facts and summarises the judgment.

It was held that the defendants were guilty of negligence in their spraying and were liable to the beekeepers for the damage they suffered.

REPORT
Of
TUTTON & OTHERS v. A.D. WALTER LTD.
[1986] 1 Q.B. 61
[Queens Bench Division: Lewes]

1984 Oct. 8, 9, 10, 11, 12   Dennis Henry Q.C.
                                          sitting as a deputy High Court judge

Negligence-Duty of care to whom?-Beekeepers-Farmer spraying crop with insecticide-Insecticide known to be harmful to bees-Whether bees trespassers-Whether farmer owing duty of care to bee keepers.

The plaintiffs kept bees near land farmed by the defendant company and upon which grew a crop of oil seed rape. The flowers of rape, although self-pollinating, were particularly attractive to bees. The crop was affected by seed weevils to a degree which justified control by spraying with an insecticide. The insecticide was known to be dangerous to bees and the advice to farmers from both government agencies and the manufacturers emphasised the need to protect bees by not spraying during the flowering period and that the insecticide was most effective when spraying took place after the flowering period. In early June, while the oil seed rape was still substantially in flower and being worked by the bees, the defendants, having given a warning only 24 hours earlier to only two of the five plaintiffs, sprayed the field with insecticide, killing the bees.

On the plaintiffs' claim for damages in negligence for the loss of their colonies of bees:-

Held, (1) that, although the defendants were carrying out a lawful activity on their land and neither invited nor needed the presence of the bees to pollinate the crop, it was unreal to divide bees into the categories of invitees, licensees or trespassers, since it was inevitable from the use to which the defendants had put the land that the bees would be present in large numbers during the flowering season; that the defendants owed a common duty of care to neighbouring bee keepers since they knew of their presence in the neighbourhood, had knowledge of the danger to bees of spraying during the flowering period and had the bee keepers in their contemplation before they began spraying; that in failing to comply with published recommendations in circumstances where a later spraying would have been more advantageous to the defendants and less damaging to the colonies of bees, the defendants had not exercised the standard of care required and, therefore, were in breach of the duty owed to the plaintiffs (post, pp. 75 F-H, 76A-F, G-77c)

Donoghue v. Stevenson [1932] A.C. 562, H.L. (Sc) applied

Herrington v. British Railways Board [1972] A.C. 877, H.L. (E) and dictum of Lord Denning M.R. in *Pannett v. P.McGuinness & Co. Ltd* [1972] 2 Q.B. 599,606-607, C.A. considered.

(2) That, although beekeepers had to accept that crops would be sprayed and should therefore take steps to minimise the dangers to their bees, the warning given by the defendants to some of the plaintiffs that the crop would be sprayed was inadequate for those plaintiffs to take the precaution of moving their hives and, therefore, they had not failed in their duty to minimise the risks to their bees (post, pp. 78 B-E, 79D-E).

Per curiam. If the bees were to be treated as being, or as analogous to, trespassers, the precautions that a landowner should take equate precisely with what the law on negligence would expect of him, so that the test under *Herrington v. British Railways Board* [1972] A.C. 877 was, on the facts, the same test, or one leading to the same conclusion (post, pp.77D-78A).

The following cases are referred to in the judgment:

Donoghue v. Stevenson [1932] A.C. 562, H.L. (Sc)

Herrington v. British Railways Board [1972] A.C. 877

Dorset Yacht Co. Ltd. v. Home Office. [1970] A.C. 1004

Pannett v. P. McGuinness & Co. Ltd. [1972] 2 Q.B. 599

The following additional cases were cited in argument:

Addie (Robert) & Sons (Collieries) Ltd. V. Dumbreck. [1929] A.C. 358

Bradford Corporation v. Pickles. [1895] A.C. 587

Cresswell v. Sirl. [1948] 1 K.B. 241.

Hamps v. Darby. [1948] 2 K.B. 311

Hollywood Silver Fox Farm Ltd. v. Emmett. [1936] 2 K.B. 468

Kearry v. Pattinson. [1939] 1 K.B. 471

Neuwith v. Over Darwen Industrial Co-operative Society. [1894] 63 L.J.Q.B. 290

O'Gorman v. O'Gorman. [1903] 2 I.R. 573

Robins v. Kennedy and Columb. [1931] N.Z.L.R. 1134

ACTION

By a statement of claim dated 10 May 1982, the plaintiffs, T .R.Tutton, Adrian Roberts, Hilary Richardson, J.Letheren and J. Donaghy, who were bee keepers in the vicinity of Hambrook near Chichester in West Sussex, claimed damages against the defendants, A.D.Walter Ltd., on the ground that they had been negligent in carrying on their business as farmers and agriculturists. The plaintiffs alleged that on 3 June 1981 the defendants, who knew or ought to have known that oil seed rape was especially attractive to bees, sprayed a field of oil seed rape in or substantially in full flower with a chemical preparation called Hostathion killing a considerable number of bees, the property of or in the possession of the plaintiffs, which were foraging in the field of oil seed rape.

The particulars of negligence were (i) spraying the crop while it was at flowering stage and/or partly or noticeably yellow and thus attractive to bees, and before the field was predominantly green; (ii) spraying the crops in spite of the manufacturer's recommendation that the oil seed rape should be sprayed "at petal fall" when the field had a predominantly green appearance; (iii) spraying the crop at flowering stage contrary to the manufacturer's instructions on the product label stating that the chemical was "dangerous to bees". "Do not apply at flowering stages"; (iv) failing to pay any or any sufficient regard to the recommendations or instructions and/or failure to take any or adequate steps to appraise themselves of the circumstances in which spraying should be carried out safely; (v) using a chemical spray which they knew, or ought to have known, was highly toxic to bees and/or failure to acquaint themselves with its toxic properties; (vi) failing to use an alternative spray of lower toxicity to bees and/or less persistence, namely Zolone, and/or failing to take any adequate steps to investigate alternative sprays; (vii) failing to pay any or any sufficient regard to published literature on crop spraying which were or ought to have been well known to the defendants and/or failing to take any or any adequate steps to appraise themselves of the circumstances in which spraying could be carried out safely; (viii) failing to give the local bee keepers and in particular the plaintiffs directly and/or through the West Sussex Bee Keepers Association adequate warning of their intention to spray the field on 3 June 1981; (ix) spraying the crop about 9.30 a.m. and 11.15 a.m. rather than during the early morning or the late evening when the bees are least active; (x) in so far as the defendants told the plaintiffs or any of them of their intention to spray, failing to heed the first and second plaintiff'' statements to the defendants' foreman, Mr. Moon, that the field was not ready for spraying on 3 June 1981 and spraying should not take place; and (xi) failing to carry out any or any proper assessment of whether the field required and/or had reached a suitable and safe stage for spraying on 3 June 1981.

Judgment for plaintifs with costs of issue on liablility. Damages to be assessed.

Counsel : Laurence Marsh (for the plaintiffs) Robert Pryor Q.C. (for the defendants)

Solicitors: Turberville & Woodbridge, Uxbridge; Blake Lapthorn, Portsmouth.

[Reported by Bernadette Miscampbell, Barrister-at-Law]

XI   **1983. England.**
TICKNER v. WHITE
Editors' Introductory Notes.

The judge said:-

The plaintiffs' counsel indicated that he did not intend to proceed on the ground of trespass, in his view quite rightly

It was accepted by both counsel that this was one of those cases where, if there was nuisance, there must also be negligence. Negligence must be established.

As to the law it was quite clear that a person was entitled to use his land in a reasonable way. That includes keeping animals.

It had been accepted that he should treat bees as domestic animals and that they were not to be regarded as *ferae naturae.*

However, one must use land reasonably and control ones property with reasonable care and without negligence. He had to decide whether this common English pastime of keeping bees was conducted in such a way as to be unreasonable.

In this particular case there was no question of a swarm. These were individual bees. He must decide (a) whether they were from Mr. White's hive (b) whether they got out because they were kept in an unreasonable place, in unreasonable numbers and in too close proximity to neighbours.

There was a question as to whether the fourteen stings were caused by Mr. White's bees. He was unable to say that he was so satisfied.

Having hives in this particular place was not unreasonable nor were there an unreasonable number of hives. He was unable to say there had been nuisance or negligence on the part of the defendant.

JUDGMENT
in the case of
TICKNER v. WHITE.
1983 TUNBRIDGE WELLS COUNTY COURT.

His Honour Judge Goodman

The following note of the judgment has been approved by the Judge:-

In this action the plaintiffs, Mr. and Mrs. Tickner, seek an injunction and damages against the defendant, Mr. White, arising out of the fact that they were both stung by bees in the summer of 1982. The claim includes allegations of nuisance and negligence and trespass. The Plaintiffs' counsel indicated that he did not intend to proceed on the ground of trespass, in my view quite rightly. It is accepted by both counsel that this is one of those cases where, if there is nuisance, there must also be negligence. Negligence must be established.

Mr. and Mrs. Tickner live at 48 Brook Mead. The property was purchased in 1968. It is in a quiet residential road and there is a garden which goes down to open land, farmland, fields and the like. When purchased there was a short garden bounded by a stream or brook across the back. In 1977 they were able to purchase some more land including a strip running behind the garden of their next-door neighbour. This strip is some thirty feet in width which Mr. and Mrs. Tickner used as a kitchen garden. As a result they had an L-shaped property.

Mr. and Mrs. Tickner are keen gardeners. I have visited the properties and there is an evident contrast between the two. Mr. and Mrs. Tickner are keen on flowers and lawns. Mr. White is not quite so interested but is interested in animals and birds. He kept chickens and small animals, no doubt for his children. Also in recent years, he has kept bees in the lower part of his garden. Mr. White has for some years been interested in beekeeping. He took up an interest in it and went to classes in 1976. By 1982 he felt sufficiently qualified to start a hive. He says, and I accept, that he would have started earlier if he had had the finance.

In April 1982 Mr. White decided to get his first hive. He got it from Barwood and purchased it with the assistance of Mr. Parsons. I should say that almost all the witnesses with the exception of Mr. Mayer have sworn affidavits in connection with an interlocutory application for an injunction. The affidavits have been admitted in evidence in the proceedings. The witnesses have supplemented their evidence and have also been cross-examined.

Mr. White, together with Mr. Parsons who had considerable experience of beekeeping, went to get his first hive on 25th April. The hive was brought back and sited fifteen feet from the boundary between the bottom of his garden and the Tickners'.

Up to then the Tickners say, and I accept, that they never had any trouble with bees or bee stings. Mr. White looked at his first hive after about a week and found it to contain a weak stock. The bees were few in number. According to Mr. Hendry, who clearly has considerable experience of bees, there were only four frames in the hive with 1500 to 2000 bees on each frame. There were an estimated 5,000 bees in the hive. It is common to find between 60,000 and 80,000 bees in a hive. The numbers go down and then build up again. This was certainly not a very full hive.

Mr. White was doubtful whether the bees would survive. He therefore thought he would unite the hive with a Lamberhurst hive which he acquired. It had no queen although there were reported to be queen cells. Mr. Hendry thought the number of bees in it were 20,000 at most.

On approximately 21st May Mr. White observed that a swarm of bees had arrived. They came from an unknown place and were on the fence between his land and the Tickners' land. He decided to hive them partly so he could add them to his stock and also because he thought something ought to be done about them. He therefore had three hives with three feet intervals between each. They were on the western side of Mr. White's garden. Three weeks later he found there was still no queen in the Lamberhurst hive and he therefore decided to split it and unite the bees with the Barwood hive and the hive having the swarm. Two weeks later he examined the two hives and found that the swarm was not as good tempered as the bees in the Barwood hive. He decided to get rid of it and destroyed the queen and united those bees with the Barwood hive.

During the period from 31st May when the swarm was hived and 11th July when Mr. White, Mr. Parsons and Mr. Hendry destroyed the queen and united the hives, Mr. and Mrs. Tickner had suffered a number of bee stings. According to Mr. Tickner between about April and July he was stung on seven occasions. On two or three occasions the dog was stung. Mrs. Tickner was also stung on eight occasions altogether she says, the first occasion being in June. This was taking place at the same time as the uniting of the hives.

The stings took place when the Tickners were at the bottom of their garden. The stings were of no real consequence to Mr. Tickner. They irritated him but they passed off. The effect on Mrs. Tickner was more serious. On the first occasion she was stung five times by five different bees. There were three stings on her face and two on her wrist. On a number of further occasions during June she suffered stings and had to have pills to bring the swelling down. The difficulty lasted some weeks. I accept that it must have been painful. She says she had an allergy. The Tickners produced no medical evidence. Mr. Mayer says that it could not have been an allergy in the strict sense of the word because she would suffer the symptoms set out in paragraph ten of his report. He is therefore satisfied that the lady did not suffer an allergy although, as I suggested, some people may react more violently than others. At the end of June having made certain complaints, the Tickners say they decided to have no more to do with the patch at the back. They say they did not use it. In cross-examination that was slightly modified. Mr. Tickner accepted it was used sometimes. A certain amount was done in that part of the garden. I have seen a photograph alleged to have been taken in May which shows potatoes and strawberries planted there. They say they used the garden one third less than they would normally have done.

There was some correspondence with regard to the matter. It was suggested that Mr. White should move the hive. He said he would do so without prejudice on the basis that the Tickners made no further claim. This was clearly designed to promote good neighbourliness but it did not succeed.

This year I held a site inspection on 27th June. Thereafter Mr. and Mrs. Tickner started to use the bottom of their garden more regularly but not after 11a.m. It is right to say that they have not been stung since last summer. It is also right to say that Mr. Cox and his family have had no problems and nor has anyone else complained.

Two things did occur this year.

Early in May a swarm of bees landed on the washing whilst Mrs. Tickner was hanging it out. She very fairly said she did not know where they came from. It is clear from Mr. White's evidence that they were not from his hive. Mr. White would have noticed if they had swarmed from his hive because bees do not return once they swarm and clearly his bees remained in the hive. I accept that that swarm was nothing to do with Mr. White. The significance of it is that the swarm must have come from somewhere else as did the bees that swarmed on to the fence in June 1982.

Early in August Mrs.Tickner and her husband came back after lunch on a Sunday. Mr. Tickner went into the garden with the dog and threw a ball. The dog returned with two bees on his back. Mr. Tickner says the dog must have been stung because he was yelping and his tail was between his legs. Again he could not say where the bees came from. It was the first time there had been bee stings since early June 1982. Heated words were exchanged.

As to the law it is quite clear that a person is entitled to use his land in a reasonable way. That includes keeping animals. It has been accepted that I should treat bees as domestic animals and that they are not to be regarded as *ferae naturae*. However, one must use land reasonably and control ones property with reasonable care and without negligence. I have to decide whether this common English pastime of keeping bees was conducted in such a way as to be unreasonable.

Obviously having animals at all can give rise to trouble with neighbours. People may have other animals that can cause damage. Provided that it occurs without negligence it must be accepted. I have to see whether there is anything in this case taking it out of the ordinary. I must also be satisfied that it was Mr. White's bees that caused the trouble.

In the case of *O'Gorman v. O'Gorman* [1903] 2 I.R. 573 Divisional Court in Ireland on Appeal, the Court upheld a Judge's finding that bees which had swarmed and landed on a horse and also stung the Plaintiff, did so in circumstances amounting to nuisance and negligence. In the judgment of Kenny J. at page 581, reference was made to the question whether the bees were kept in an unreasonable manner, in an unreasonable place or in unreasonable numbers.

In this particular case there is no question of a swarm. These are individual bees. I must decide (a) whether they were from Mr. White's hive (b) whether they got out because they were kept in an unreasonable place, in unreasonable numbers and in too close proximity to neighbours.

In the case I have referred to there was no argument as to whether the bees were the defendant's. It is interesting that in the paper given by Master Sir Kenneth Swan he raised a question as to whether the court was right to have found that the bees were the defendant's. He pointed out that this was an important factor to be considered before anything else.

At first blush it seems likely that the bees in this case were Mr. White's. The bees were on the Tickners' property. They had never been there before. The Tickners were never stung before. However it is not quite so simple as that. I have heard evidence from Mr. Mayer, Mr. Parsons and Mr. Hendry, all of whom are very experienced, to the effect that when bees come out to forage they come straight out of the hive and rise. They are unlikely to be in the immediate vicinity of the hive. If they go along at ground level no doubt they may well sting. I must consider what precautions were taken to see that the bees would take off and clear anything in the immediate vicinity. Mr. White tells me that when he purchased the property he planted conifers. At one side of the garden they were 6-8 feet high. On the Tickners' side some were only four feet high. He also had chicken wire netting and green mesh placed at points near outlets which would stop the bees going straight ahead. I am satisfied that there was a proper barrier here that would prevent the bees getting through. The vast majority of the bees would have been up in the air and away. In any event Mr. Mayer's evidence is that they forage all over. Mr. Hendry and Mr. Parsons gave evidence that there are forty to fifty hives in the area and it is therefore highly likely that the bees around were bees from elsewhere rather than from Mr. White's hive.

Mr. Mayer said: "I cannot say if the bees came from Mr. White's hive. All I can say is that bees like to forage at a distance and it is therefore unlikely that the bees were from Mr. White's garden." I pressed him further but he maintained that he did not think it was likely that they were Mr. White's bees.

It is a matter for me to decide what I make of his evidence. It is clearly well informed evidence. Mr. Mayer has seen the situation as it is today and says that it is satisfactory. On the evidence I do not think I can decide it was much different a year ago. The screening would therefore have caused the bees to rise and go away. There is a question as to whether the fourteen stings were caused by Mr. White's bees. I am unable to say that I am so satisfied.

Even if I were, I would still have to be satisfied that they were kept unreasonably. It is significant to note that the number of bees and hives is really relatively small. I cannot put a total on it. There appears to have been some 5,000 bees plus the contents of the third hive. In the *O'Gorman* case there were twenty to thirty hives. In the Canadian case of *Lucas v. Pettit* there were 160 hives. I do not overlook the other case of *Parker v. Reynolds* (Times 17th December 1906). In that case there were ten hives against the fence where the neighbour had his property and the bees got into the house.

I do not think that the three weeks during which there were three hives and the period when there were two and then one means that the bees were kept in unreasonable numbers. Was it an unreasonable place? It was near a vegetable patch, it was not near a house. In my view it is not an unreasonable place. The Tickners have not used the strip since the stings and they have had no trouble since summer 1982. As far as the dog is concerned, the dog did tend to snap says Mr. White. I think a dog would. I think getting stung is an occupational hazard of living in a rural setting. Having hives in this particular place was not unreasonable nor were there an unreasonable number of hives.

Was there an appreciable danger of the Tickners getting stung on their land? Mrs. Tickner did get stung and did suffer quite badly. Mr. Mayer says that she may be frightened of bees. Adrenalin is therefore pumped into the bloodstream. In those circumstances bees may sting. Mr. Mayer has given the only expert evidence and I must consider that as being possible. The Tickners are clearly satisfied that their stings were Mr. White's fault. It was unfortunate. They have not been stung since and I hope it will not happen in the future.

I am unable to say there has been nuisance or negligence on the part of the defendant. I must dismiss the claim. In concluding I would say that Mr. Mayer has pointed out that he does not think it would be of assistance if the hive was moved but if it is thought that it will help Mrs. Tickner, Mr .White may think that it would be a prudent move to take. I must however emphasise that the failure to move the hive is not in my judgment an act of negligence or nuisance.

On Counsel's application the Judge awarded costs on Scale 2 to the defendant.

XII   1991. England
NEWARK & SHERWOOD DISTRICT COUNCIL v.
A BEEKEEPER

Editors Introductory Notes.

The account of this case is most important for beekeepers as it illustrates how neighbours may in the future try to obtain injunctions to prevent a beekeeper from keeping bees.

A summary of some of the clauses of the Environmental Protection Act 1990 are given at the end of the report .

The problem for the beekeeper is that the procedure from the neighbour's point of view and that of the local authority is very simple and cheap while taking the matter to the County Court or High Court can be very expensive and take some time.

It is advisable for beekeepers to know in outline the procedure that the local authority can adopt and realise that if an enforcement notice is served application must be made within the limited time to the Magistrates Court if it is desired to have it set aside.

If a neighbour is likely to apply to the Local Authority it is very helpful if the beekeeper gets officials of his local association to inspect and give a report on whether he is keeping an unreasonable number of bees, in an unreasonable place or in an unreasonable manner or not. Full plans can be most helpful.

NEWARK & SHERWOOD DISTRICT COUNCIL v.
A BEEKEEPER
APRIL 1991
Summary of Note supplied by the Council's Department of Housing and Environmental Health.

Newark and Sherwood District Council Environmental Health Section first received complaints concerning bees during the summer of 1989, although complainants ultimately alleged they had been experiencing problems associated with bees since 1985/86.

Primarily the complaints concerned:- (1) Deposits of a yellow waxy substance on windows, washing and vehicles with problems being experienced with their removal, (2) disturbance, causing a loss of enjoyment of property and gardens and (3) incidents of stinging.

During June 1986, bees started to swarm in gardens closest to the location of the hives and residents reported being stung on many occasions during 1988/89 as the number of bees kept at the site increased.

Initial enquiries revealed that an estimated 40 hives in various states of repair were situated on a small rectangular plot of land approximately 105 square metres in area. Not all of the hives were inhabited. The hive site was located within the residential area of a small village and was bounded on two sides by the gardens of three bungalows with a 2 - 3 metre high Privet hedge separating the properties from the hive site. A public footpath ran alongside the remaining two sides of the plot.

Complainants were interviewed as to their experiences with the bees. A resident of one of the three bungalows adjacent described her garden as "a sea of bees" and that the enjoyment of her patio area and pond was prevented by substantial numbers of bees, in their hundreds on occasions, being present in her garden.

Because of the disturbing effect of the bees on local residents and persons using the public footpath, and the incidents of stinging and spotting caused by bee deposits, an abatement notice under Section 93 of the Public Health Act 1936 was served on the owner of the bees, (who was also the owner of the site) on the 15th March 1990, requiring him to remove the bees, all hives and associated equipment from the site within 14 days. The recipient contested the notice asking for proof that the nuisance was caused by his bees.

The owner failed to comply with the abatement notice within the prescribed time and in addition the Environmental Health Section continued to receive nuisance complaints. The matter was therefore referred to the Council's solicitors for the purpose of obtaining a Nuisance Order in the Magistrates Court.

In preparing a case, Counsel's advice was sought and the following advice obtained:-

1. Bees are animals for the purposes of section 92 (1) (b) of the Public Health Act 1936. Although there is no definition contained within the Act or in the Animals Act 1971, dictionary definitions led to this conclusion. Civil cases relating to negligence for harm caused by animals and in particular bees also reaffirmed this view.

2. Satisfactory evidence would be required including

(a) Evidence of an expert to show that the number of bees on the site was excessive. Initially the support of the local bee keeping fraternity was not forthcoming and therefore the Council relied on Guidance Notes issued by the Ministry of Agriculture Fisheries and Food (Advisory Leaflet 283) and the Bee-keepers Association (Advisory Leaflet 31).

(b) Evidence from neighbours as to the degree of nuisance caused either by stinging, disturbance or through spotting of furnishings, fixtures and fittings by the yellow waxy substance.

3. Details of a number of legal law reports on negligence and nuisance caused by bees including,

(a) *O'Gorman v. O'Gorman.* [1903] 2 Ir.R. 573 (Negligence)

(b) *Robins v. Kennedy and Columb* [1931] N.Z.L.R. 1134 (Nuisance)

(c) *Farrer v. Nelson* (1885)15 Q.B.D. 258 (Nuisance)

(d) *Selegman v. Docker* [1949] 1 Ch 53 (Nuisance)

(e) *Peech v. Best* [1931] 1 K.B.1 (Nuisance)

(f) *Stearn v. Prentice Bros.* [1919] 1 KB 394 (Nuisance)

On the 3rd August 1990 a Nuisance Order was made by Newark and Southwell Magistrates Court requiring the owner "to remove said bees and all hives and associated equipment from the said land and to abate or prevent recurrence of said nuisance within 28 days".

No effort was made to comply with the order in spite of further letters from the Council and subsequently information was laid before the Magistrates Court in respect of the owner's failure to meet the terms of the nuisance order.

However during October 1990 the bee keeper concerned was granted leave to appeal out of time against the making of the Nuisance Order to Nottingham Crown Court. The proceedings for failure to comply with the Order were held in abeyance by the Magistrates Court pending the outcome of the appeal.

By way of further preparation for the appeal, evidence was sought from ten residents who were willing to appear and give evidence. Maps and diagrams were produced showing locations of complainants in relation to the hive site and the location of other known bee-keepers in the village. Photographs were also prepared. In addition advice was sought from two independent bee-keepers from outside the District Council's area who both concluded that the land was inappropriate for the siting of hives. The exact number of bees was difficult to determine although it was estimated that in high summer it was likely there would be in excess of 2 million bees hived within the site, assuming the presence of 40 bee colonies.

On the 14th March 1991 the appeal was heard at Nottingham Crown Court. After the appearance of only three of the Council's witnesses the appellant withdrew his appeal and the Judge ordered the removal of the bees from the site within 28 days although she amended the order to delete the requirement to remove hives and associated equipment from the land.

Costs of £500 were awarded against the appellant to add to the costs of £200 which had been incurred in the Magistrates Court.

This case was lengthy, costly and certainly more complex than would have appeared necessary on face value. There were probably two reasons for this; firstly, the fact that the owner of the bees was particularly reluctant to co-operate and secondly because the case was the first to be taken of its kind and in that sense new ground was being trodden for the first time.

Notwithstanding the confirmation of the Order by the Crown Court the beekeeper had not at the date of the writing of the note removed all the bees from the land and the Council was accordingly considering removing the bees from the land in default in addition to reinstating the Magistrates Court proceedings for non compliance with the order.

XIII   Extracts from
Environmental Protection Act 1990
together with some Notes.

Section 79. ...the following matters constitute "statutory nuisances" for the purposes of this Part, that is to say -   (f) any animal kept in such a place or manner as to be prejudicial to health or a nuisance;
[It would seem that it is not necessary to prove that a nuisance is prejudicial to health; it is sufficient to show that it interferes with personal comfort. The distinction between public and private nuisance is immaterial for the purposes of this section. see *Betts v. Penge Urban District Council,* [1942] 2 All E.R. 61. Interference with the enjoyment of neighbouring property is a prerequisite.]

Section 80. (1) Where a local authority is satisfied that a statutory nuisance exists, or is likely to occur or recur, in the area of the authority, the local authority shall serve a notice ("an abatement notice") imposing all or any of the following requirements -

(a) requiring the abatement of the nuisance or prohibiting or restricting its occurrence or recurrence.

(b) requiring the execution of such works, and the taking of such other steps, as may be necessary for any of those purposes

and the notice shall specify the time or times within which the requirements of the notice are to be complied with.

(3) The person served with the notice may appeal against the notice to a magistrates court within the period of twenty one days beginning with the date on

which he was served with the notice.

(4) If a person on whom an abatement notice is served, without reasonable excuse, contravenes or fails to comply with any requirement or prohibition imposed by the notice, he shall be guilty of an offence.

[It is essential for the beekeeper to act quickly and either accept the Notice and act upon it or appeal to the Magistrates' Court within the time limit]

Section 81. (3) Where an abatement notice has not been complied with the local authority may, whether or not they take proceedings for an offence under section 80 (4) above, abate the nuisance and do whatever may be necessary in execution of the notice.

Section 82. (1) A magistrates' court may act under this section on a complaint made by any person on the ground that he is aggrieved by the existence of a statutory nuisance.

(2) If the magistrates' court is satisfied that the alleged nuisance exists, or that although abated it is likely to recur on the same premises, the court shall make an order for either or both of the following purposes -

(a) requiring the defendant to abate the nuisance, within a time specified in the order, and to execute any works necessary for that purpose;

(b) prohibiting a recurrence of the nuisance, and requiring the defendant, within a time specified in the order, to execute any works necessary to prevent the recurrence .

[Under this section the neighbour can take action by making a complaint himself and he does not need the support of the local authority.]

Appendix 1: Table of Cases

Cases included in Appendix 2 are not all included in this Table

Appendix 2.

Table of other beekeeping cases.

Ammons v. Kellogg. (1925) 137 Miss. 551

Bradley & Bradley v. Hall & Garland. (1966) Bee Craft. Jan 1966: 6

Devon County Council v. West Country Honey Farms Ltd. (1976) Bee Craft 1976 230

Ellis v. Mitchell (1948) Malton Gazette

Hallett v. Jones (1935) LXXX Law Journal 173

Harris v. Elder (1893) 57 J.P. 553

Jackson v. Wade (1987) Birmingham County Court. His Hon. Judge Harold Wilson

Jennings v. Hildyard (1912) The Yorkshire Herald. July 11th

McKay v. Davey. (1913) XXVIII Ontario L.R. 322.

McStay v. Morrisey [1949] 83 I. L. T. R. 28

Mills and others v. Bolingbroke (1979) Chelmsford County Court. His Hon. Judge Turner

Olmsted v. Rich (1889) 3 Silv. 6 N.Y. Sup 826

Parsons v. Manser (1903) 119 Iowa 88

People v. McComber (1953) 133 N.Y.S. 2d 407

Quantrill v. Spragge (1907) 71 J.P. Jo. 425

Tellier v. Pelland (1873), 5 R.L.N.S., 61

Walters and others v. Cuthbertson (1982) Taunton County Court. His Hon. Judge Best

Wenlock v. Curtis (1929) 73 Solicitors' Journal 861

BIBLIOGRAPHY

American Law Reports. (1987) Beekeeping - Regulations. *55 ALR. 4th*: 1224.

Ashton-Cross, D.I.C. (1953) Liability in Roman Law for Damage caused by Animals *Cambridge Law Journal* 11. 395-403

Blackstone, (1766) *Commentaries on the Laws of England.* Book II Ch 25. 389-395

British Beekeepers' Association (N.D.) *Bees and Neighbours.* Advisory Leaflet No. 31

Buckley, (1981) *The Law of Nuisance.* (London)

Burr, Judge Leslie.(1945) Laws relating to Bees. *The ABC and XYZ of Bee culture.*(Ohio) 458-464

Campbell, C.P. (1924) *The Law pertaining to the Honeybee* (Madison, Wisconsin) pp. 88.

Cohn, E.J. (1939) Bees and the Law. *The Law Quarterly Review* CCXVIII: 289-294

Devon Apicultural Research Group.(1992) *Beeway Code* (Ivybridge, Devon) : pp. 12

Digest, The. Vol. 2. Animals: 324. Butterworths, London

Doutt, R. L. (1959) The Case of the Trespassing Bees. *Bulletin of the Entomological.Society of America* 5 (3): 93-97

Field-Fisher, T.G. (1964) *Animals and the Law.*(London) pp.140

Frimston, J.D.(1966) Bee-keeping and the Law. *Central Association of Beekeepers. London:* pp. 15

Frimston, J.D. (1991) Bee-keepers and their Neighbours. *Central Association of Beekeepers.* London : pp. 15

Gooding, Stanley. (1952) Bee-Keeping and the Law. *Central Association of Beekeepers,* London : pp.8

Halsbury's Laws of England (1991) 4th Ed. Reissue Vol 2 :Animals: 84

Halsbury's Laws of England (1980) 4th Edition. Vol 34. Negligence: 1. Nuisance: 100

Harrison, D.B. (1978) Keeping Bees as Nuisance. 88 *ALR 3d*: 992-1000

Harrison, D.B. (1978) Liability for Injury or damage caused by Bees. 86 *ALR3d*: 829-838

Hill, D.C. (1964) Liability for Animals. *Law Journal* CXIV : 300-303

Jelf, Master E.A. (1939) Bees. *Encyclopaedia of the Laws of England.* 218 - 219

Jenkins, Dafydd (1986) *The Law of Hywel Dda.* (Llandysul, Wales) pp. 426

Law Journal (1935) The Law of Beekeeping. *The Law Journal* LXXX: 173-174

Loring, M. (1981) *Bees and the Law.* (Hamilton, Illinois) pp. 128

Macrory, R. (1982) *Nuisance.* (London) : pp.110

North, P.M. (1972) *The Modern Law of Animals.* (London) pp. 230

Park, R.B. (1990) The Social Obligations of Beekeepers. *Bee World* 71 (1) :8-11

Read, H.E. (1933) Animals-Ferae Naturae and Domitae Naturae. *The Canadian Bar Revue* 3:216-222

Sandys-Winch, G.(1984) *Animal Law.* (London) pp.260

Solicitors Journal. (1945) Bees. *Solicitors Journal.* March 10th: 113 - 114

Solicitors Journal. (1952) Liability for Damage done by Animals. *Solicitors Journal* 96: 653-654

Swan, Sir Kenneth. (1956) A Receiver of Stolen Property. *Hon. Society of the Middle Temple.* London: pp21

W, C.A. (1939) Animals-Bees-Property-Right to pursue. *The Canadian Bar Review.* 17: 130-139.

Williams, Glanville. (1939) *Liability for Animals* (Cambridge)